Palgrave Studies in Literary Anthropology

Series Editors
Deborah Reed-Danahay
Department of Anthropology
The State University of New York at Buffalo
Buffalo, NY, USA

Helena Wulff
Department of Social Anthropology
Stockholm University
Stockholm, Sweden

This series explores new ethnographic objects and emerging genres of writing at the intersection of literary and anthropological studies. Books in this series are grounded in ethnographic perspectives and the broader cross-cultural lens that anthropology brings to the study of reading and writing. The series explores the ethnography of fiction, ethnographic fiction, narrative ethnography, creative nonfiction, memoir, autoethnography, and the connections between travel literature and ethnographic writing.

More information about this series at
http://www.palgrave.com/gp/series/15120

Lawrence J. Taylor
Tales from the Desert Borderland

Photographs by Maeve Hickey

Lawrence J. Taylor
Maynooth University
Co. Kildare, Ireland

Photographs by
Maeve Hickey
artist, photographer
www.maevehickey.com

Palgrave Studies in Literary Anthropology
ISBN 978-3-030-35132-8   ISBN 978-3-030-35133-5 (eBook)
https://doi.org/10.1007/978-3-030-35133-5

© The Editor(s) (if applicable) and The Author(s), under exclusive licence to Springer Nature Switzerland AG 2020
This work is subject to copyright. All rights are solely and exclusively licensed by the Publisher, whether the whole or part of the material is concerned, specifically the rights of translation, reprinting, reuse of illustrations, recitation, broadcasting, reproduction on microfilms or in any other physical way, and transmission or information storage and retrieval, electronic adaptation, computer software, or by similar or dissimilar methodology now known or hereafter developed.
The use of general descriptive names, registered names, trademarks, service marks, etc. in this publication does not imply, even in the absence of a specific statement, that such names are exempt from the relevant protective laws and regulations and therefore free for general use.
The publisher, the authors and the editors are safe to assume that the advice and information in this book are believed to be true and accurate at the date of publication. Neither the publisher nor the authors or the editors give a warranty, expressed or implied, with respect to the material contained herein or for any errors or omissions that may have been made. The publisher remains neutral with regard to jurisdictional claims in published maps and institutional affiliations.

Cover illustration: photograph by Maeve Hickey

This Palgrave Macmillan imprint is published by the registered company Springer Nature Switzerland AG.
The registered company address is: Gewerbestrasse 11, 6330 Cham, Switzerland

Series Preface

Palgrave Studies in Literary Anthropology publishes explorations of new ethnographic objects and emerging genres of writing at the intersection of literary and anthropological studies. Books in this series are grounded in ethnographic perspectives and the broader cross-cultural lens that anthropology brings to the study of reading and writing. By introducing work that applies an anthropological approach to literature, whether drawing on ethnography or other materials in relation to anthropological and literary theory, this series moves the conversation forward not only in literary anthropology, but in general anthropology, literary studies, cultural studies, sociology, ethnographic writing and creative writing. The "literary turn" in anthropology and critical research on world literatures share a comparable sensibility regarding global perspectives.

Fiction and autobiography have connections to ethnography that underscore the idea of the author as ethnographer and the ethnographer as author. Literary works are frequently included in anthropological research and writing, as well as in studies that do not focus specifically on literature. Anthropologists take an interest in fiction and memoir set in their field locations, and produced by "native" writers, in order to further their insights into the cultures and contexts they research. Experimental genres in anthropology have benefitted from the style and structure of fiction and autoethnography, as well as by other expressive forms ranging from film and performance art to technology, especially the internet and social media. There are renowned fiction writers who trained as anthropologists, but moved on to a literary career. Their anthropologically inspired work is a common sounding board in literary anthropology. In the endeavor to foster writing skills in different genres, there are now courses on ethnographic writing, anthropological writing genres, experimental writing, and even creative writing taught by anthropologists. And increasingly, literary and reading communities are attracting anthropological attention, including an engagement with issues of how to reach a wider audience.

Palgrave Studies in Literary Anthropology publishes scholarship on the ethnography of fiction and other writing genres, the connections between travel literature and ethnographic writing, and internet writing. It also publishes creative work such as ethnographic fiction, narrative ethnography, creative nonfiction, memoir, and autoethnography. Books in the series include monographs and edited collections, as well as shorter works that appear as Palgrave Pivots. This series aims to reach a broad audience among scholars, students and a general readership.

Deborah Reed-Danahay and Helena Wulff
Co-Editors, Palgrave Studies in Literary Anthropology

Advisory Board
Ruth Behar, University of Michigan
Don Brenneis, University of California, Santa Cruz
Regina Bendix, University of Göttingen
Mary Gallagher, University College Dublin
Kirin Narayan, Australian National University
Nigel Rapport, University of St Andrews
Ato Quayson, University of Toronto
Julia Watson, Ohio State University

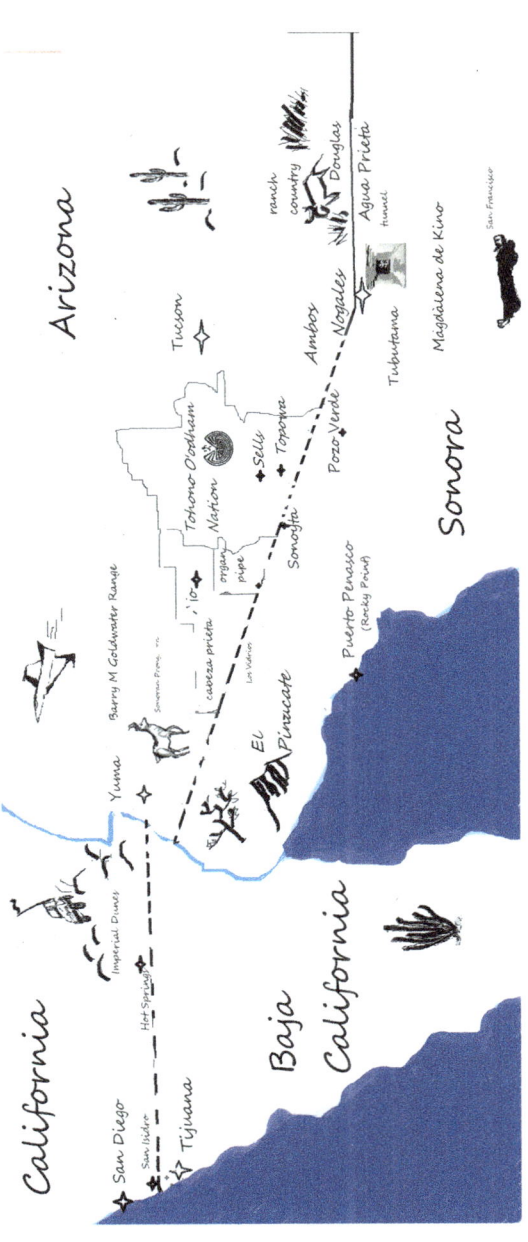

Fig. 1 Map. (Drawing by Lawrence Taylor)

Foreword

Borders cannot be fenced; lives are seamless. This is the prevailing ethos of *Tales from the Desert Borderland*, a timely and important work of ethnographic fiction written by a renowned observer and promiscuous itinerant of the western borderlands of Mexico and the US, Lawrence Taylor. Through these richly textured and entwined stories about *fronterizos* (inhabitants of the border), Taylor invites us to reexamine our own stereotypes and tropes about a people and place we need to understand more fully and with more familiarity than distance. In these stories, the reader will encounter not the usual suspects or dualisms that permeate most of the recent literature on the border: alien and citizen; The Wall; desert tombs; illegal and legal; or the latest border policing technology, lurking drones. For as much as these works are critical of the consequences of America's immigration and border control policies, they tend toward what the anthropologist Nicholas De Genova has termed "border spectacle," a performance of legal exclusion whereby repetitive images and language work to produce a theater of "illegality" and inhumanity. In Taylor's book, though, there is no spectacle to watch, no performance of illegality to witness. Through ethnographic fiction, we, instead, are immersed in the everyday and interconnected lives of *fronterizos* in which struggle is endured, plots of revenge are sometimes hatched, and small joys are found. These are the border stories we all need to read.

Lawrence Taylor and I have traversed these same desert border spaces and border towns at different times, but have arrived at similar sensibilities about the past and present of the region. Nearly twenty years ago, I first came to the Arizona-Sonora borderlands as a wide-eyed, first-generation, Chicanx graduate student looking for histories of the nonspectacular, ones that more closely corresponded to family reminiscences about the region and its people than those in the academic literature I had been reading, many of which rang hollow. While plying between the native lands of my maternal family—from Magdalena de Kino to Cananea, Sonora, through Douglas, Bisbee, and Tucson, Arizona—I, like Taylor, came to understand these spaces as more fluid than rigid, as more landscapes of liminality than a "terrain of terror" enacted by officious policing and effectual segregation. I wrote about this less-familiar and less-spectacular world in my first book about Chinese *fronterizos* at the borderlands of Arizona, California, and Mexico because this omission from borderlands history did not square with my knowledge of the region, which resided in the everyday, in anecdotes, and in places where individuals created community amid a well-policed border line. For a time, I relied on my own neighborhood experiences, the transmission of family stories and the pursuit of hunches that were supported in literary interventions, ethnography and cultural geography, which proved to be as effective in reconstructing this story of the past as did a small collection of historians' essays.

What I found in this turn-of-the-twentieth-century history of the Arizona-Sonora borderlands were relationships grounded in loose kinship lines and tight neighborhood bonds that organized and sustained social and cultural interaction among *fronterizos*. In often indirect ways, a wide range of collective practices deepened relationships among *fronterizos* and preserved a sense of social fluidity that worked against a hardened national border. *Tales* begins and ends with these same sensibilities about the region. It moves with a suppleness that sets aside the spectacle of exclusion for stories of interconnection and entwined fates that I find compelling and true to the everyday lives of *fronterizos* past and present.

Tales from the Desert Borderland takes place mostly in towns that dot the Arizona and Sonora line and in a few to the west of the region. Taylor's stories are as striking and richly textured as the desert dunes they surround.

On balance, they abandon thick morality and strained and conjured disclosures for unexpected relationships and unpredictable, but plausible outcomes. Yet as dramatic and unforgiving as these topographical and political badlands are, they never overtake the human drama played out within them. Neither is the border ever erased nor are the ironic and sometimes violent ambitions of Mexican American border patrol agents softened. Achieving this balance is no small order. It is first evidenced in the opening chapter, "Machaca," that pairs two unexpectedly compatible but still oddly coupled border agents, Orozco and Clark. We see Clark, a former surfer from San Diego, wrestle with the use of aggressive deterrence his superior, Orozco, reflexively adopts, reaping the rewards of quick promotion and social acceptance among middle-class, Anglo border residents.

There are also some heartbreaking scenes here that hang in different balance, as in "Love and Lettuce," when Concha, a recent border crosser and erstwhile vendor of *raspados* (sugary, iced cones) turned field worker, loses her sweetheart, Pete, to an alluring and calculating rival, Diana Tejera. The betrayal was too much to bear, and Concha plotted a sweet revenge. There are also stories about financial and human desperation in "NAFTA" as Ned and Ruby, two cash-strapped Canadian snowbirds, embark on their maiden human-smuggling voyage. Fumbling and panicky, they turn to the precocious Lalo, a homeless "tweener" turned *pollero* (literally "chicken herder," but in this context, human smuggler of unauthorized immigrants or "chickens"). There is also an occult storytelling of the life of Chico, a biracial Tohono O'odham who overcomes his fecklessness in time to wash off the lingering sins of his dead mother, Sheila Cassidy. The past, for Chico, ceases its beguiling tricks and becomes, for him and his departed mother, a circumstance to be reconciled by mundane and fantastical actions.

Before *Tales from the Desert Borderland*, my preferred Taylor narrative intervention was *Tunnel Kids*, a stark coming-of-age account of homeless street kids who eke out their existence in the drainage tunnels connecting both Nogales (*ambos* Nogales). For this reason, I was delighted that Taylor returned to the tunnel kids in the final chapter of *Tales*, but this time the wits and *ganas* (will) of child survival were filtered, of course, through ethnographic fiction. Taylor writes this final chapter as if to hurl his readers into a tunnel of interconnected fates. Lalo of "NAFTA" reappears, as does Orozco of "Machaca," both to simultaneously steer their respective crews into a vortex of danger. What that peril was exactly, we are left to grapple with as Taylor ends *Tales* with an abrupt cut-to-black, Sopranos-like ending. Despite the ambiguity of the final scene, it jars us into a clear conclusion: we all must grapple with the consequences of confounding actions that are meant to sever the entwined lives of those residing at and traversing through the US-Mexico borderlands.

This is not the first work of nuance by Lawrence Taylor. An anthropologist by training, Taylor has penned six books, including *Tales at the Desert Borderland*, on immigration and religion spanning the disparate geographies of Ireland, Dutch America, and the US-Mexico border. That each work differs widely in terms of time and place and people and methodology is a testament to Taylor's intellectual eclecticism as well as a trademark diffidence of his own closeness to and distance from the people he writes about. In *Tales of the Desert Borderland* Taylor foregrounds this, I believe, by juxtaposing Maeve Hickey's (always) evocative photography with ethnographic fiction. This approach, in essence, works to transgress both academic disciplinary boundaries and the line between real and unreal. He deploys a literary borderlands rhetoric—a third space—from which rituals, wildlife, and human life animate a hermeneutic of a world in-between.

There is much in *Tales* that will attract readers from different audiences: fans of literary fiction on the American West; casual but constant readers of the borderlands; college students; humanists and social scientists; and anyone looking for vibrant writing and great excitements that match her /his/their personal knowledge of the border, and then some. I, myself, see that *Tales* will take new center stage in my undergraduate-level courses on immigration, Latinx history, and Chicanx history, as it easily lends itself to my Freirean-influenced teaching and learning philosophy. I approach student learning as a transformative experience, such that students are placed intellectually as co-producers of knowledge, thus equipping them with the tools to see history as directly relevant to their own lives. *Tales* easily lends itself to this purpose, placing my students, many of whom are *fronterizos*, immigrants, and first-generation Latinx college students, at the center of their own learning. I believe that integrating

Tales into history courses—and those of the humanistic social sciences—will encourage students and instructors to ponder the myriad possibilities *Tales* proposes for the present-day and future borderlands.

Lawrence Taylor has emerged as an important public intellectual and as one of North America's and Europe's most powerful storytellers of the Arizona-Sonora borderlands. Through *Tales from the Desert Borderland* you will find the mundane, the unpredictable, the tragic and sublime, and the interconnected, all of which work to counter one of the most enduring myths in American history—that the US border with Mexico has always been and will always be a well-defined, stable entity. No doubt, present-day nativist rhetoric and restrictionist border control policies, coupled with an oblivion of history north of the line, reinforce such a view. Yet, as *Tales* reminds us, this is nothing but well short of the truth. Taylor's work, like any evocative, humanistic reflection about the region, moves the readers from useless tropes and binaries to a literary rendering where strategies, practices, and adjustments steady the distrust borderlands may harbor toward one another. In the end, common ground based on common humanity is the necessary starting point from which to rethink America's current border control solutions of detention, deportation, and zero tolerance. And I cannot think of a more hopeful way to begin such a reconceptualization than by reading and teaching *Tales from the Desert Borderland.*

Fronteriza and Associate Professor Grace Peña Delgado
Department of History
University of California
Santa Cruz, CA, USA

Preface

In the fateful September of 2001 artist Maeve Hickey and I left Ireland for another period of fieldwork on the Arizona/Sonora border. *Tunnel Kids*, our book on the lives of Nogales street kids, was out and *Ambos Nogales: Intimate Portraits of the US/Mexico Border* was in press. Now we hoped to turn our attention to the great expanse of desert lands that stretched west from those Arizona/Sonora towns to the Pacific Ocean. Increasing enforcement in the cities had pushed the migrants into these unforgiving sands, and now the collapsing trade towers seemed to throw a deepening shadow of insecurity over the entire border.

Though an "empty quarter" on the map—one might imagine a vast unpeopled wilderness wasteland of sand, rock and cactus—we knew it was alive with folks on the move. There were of course thousands of migrants crossing the punishing desert to seek new lives in the promised land. But they were not alone. There was a growing number of both humanitarian volunteer groups there to help them and bands of vigilantes there to stop them. There were even locals crossing the line "in the other direction," traveling south to a Catholic shrine in Mexico, and yet others on a different sort of spiritual quest, attempting to "leave no trace" on personal journeys through the wilderness. Finally, there were the myriad agents of the federal government, not only Border Patrol and Customs, but also Park Rangers, protecting the border or managing the huge swaths of public lands in the form of national parks and monuments, wildlife refuges, and military bombing ranges through which all these sacred and secular pilgrims moved.

I was struck by the conflicting realities of these various constituencies, and perhaps because I was coming from Europe, by what seemed the distinctively American character of a conflict that went well beyond politics. Each group was on a moral mission, not only in pursuit of a political cause, but to define America (no less) on its contested edge. Led by moral entrepreneurs, they were performing rival moral geographies, inscribing them on the landscape itself with staged dramas of movement and blockade. How, I wondered, to conduct "fieldwork" among such an array of subject populations, and across such a daunting space? This called for a new version of what anthropologists like to call (following George Marcus's example) multi-sited fieldwork. As for Maeve, she is an artist and always open to adventure and the unexpected.

Our practical answer was an Isuzu Trooper and a tent trailer. Over the next decade we spent months at a time moving between and with everyone from Border Patrol to migrants, from *Humane Borders* to the *Minuteman Project*. We even walked for days through the desert with Native American pilgrims to the shrine of San Francisco Xavier in Magdalena de Kino, Mexico. For me, this work resulted in a series of articles exploring conflicting moral geographies (see www.nuim.academia.edu/LTaylor), and for Maeve, a rich corpus of photographs and assemblage/sculpture, presented over the years in photographic and mixed-media exhibitions on both religious and secular pilgrims (see www.maevehickey.com).

But we weren't always in motion. Over those years we came to rest—for weeks or months at a time—in a range of distinctive, deeply rooted or fragile and ephemeral, communities. They included not only Mexican and Mexican American villages and neighborhoods, but also Native American reservations, defunct resorts, decaying mining towns, ranches, and snowbird trailer parks. Each of these was in many ways a unique world with a cast of idiosyncratic characters engaged in the dramas of everyday life, but all were profoundly shaped by their shared natural and human environment: the desert and the border. While many of these places had no obvious role to play in my original ethnographic quest, they certainly provoked my imagination and I found myself seeking ways to capture their particular flavor, and the irony and humor as well as tragedy of the lives that unfolded (and sometimes unraveled) within them. That was the immediate genesis of the short stories before you.

The stories are fiction. Whether they are ethnographic fiction depends on your definition of the genre. If genre it is. According to Tobias Hecht's reasonable formulation, "Ethnographic fiction is a form that blends the fact-gathering research of an anthropologist with the storytelling imagination of a fiction writer ... it aims to depict a world that could be as it is told and that was discovered through anthropological research" (Hecht, *After Life: An Ethnographic Novel*, Duke University Press, 2006, p. 8). That definition seems to include both method and intention: one begins with standard ethnographic, participant-observer "fact gathering," but then deploys those facts in the creation of something that looks like a narrative ethnography, but is fictional. Often, the same author assumes academic authority in her/his nonfictional accounts of the same place/people. In that context, the "could be" of the fictional account seems to claim that "it might as well be true." For anyone insecure about the place of anthropology and ethnography in the world of social science "knowledge," this can be a worrisome inference. For me, I will admit to being less concerned with policing that line, and more interested in the varied ways in which I might be able to engage with and represent the world. But I also find that the relation between these stories and my work as an anthropologist—in terms of both method and intention—is more complicated and even elusive than the designation "ethnographic fiction" may imply. So, permit me to retrace my steps.

Like so many New Yorkers of my generation, I am the grandchild of middle and eastern European Jewish immigrants. I was brought up in an essentially atheist household but with a definite, though contradictory and confused, sense of identity, no doubt much accentuated by a change of our family's name along with a move to a small town where there were very few of "us." My early sense of being an "outsider" only strengthened over subsequent years (even to the extent of eventually becoming an Irish citizen and resident), and perhaps it was the perceived lack of cultural content in my own family that turned my gaze on the lives of nearby "others." Which is to say that an anthropological sensibility and an ethnographic perspective were for me "natural" or at least "comfortable" and found expression, perhaps ironically if logically, in the narrative and intellectual strains of my ancestors. Those inclinations may have been behind my strong attraction to and comfort with the similar cultural traits I found among the Irish, who, it can sometimes seem, survive collective and individual disaster by focusing, with black humor and self-irony, on the rich narrative it will provide. At least this is the story about myself that I have come to believe at this point in my life. Anthropology has given a shape to my alienation, which I have for the most part embraced and whose development I even encouraged in my students, always asking them to try not only to make the "strange" familiar, but equally the "familiar" strange.

The trajectory of my writing has also been profoundly influenced by my collaboration with artist Maeve Hickey, with whom I have produced three books treating the borderlands region in which these stories take place. There is no doubt that working alongside an artist has constantly challenged my perceptions, encouraged other strategies of engaging with and representing human experience, and liberated and licensed my desire to see and write as an artist as well as an anthropologist. Thus, my share of our books abandoned the usual academic language and armature and is best classed as "creative nonfiction." From there to fiction, as the Irish say, is not a million miles.

The stories were often suggested by real individuals who seemed to embody some of the core features of people and place, and who were combined or in other ways transmuted into such characters as Orozco of "Machaca," "NAFTA," and "The Tunnel," Chico of "Endangered Species" and "Burying Sheila Cassidy," Kastenbader, Viola and Lucy of "Endangered Species," and Gilberto of "Ranch Rescue."

Other tales grew from observed dramas. For example, we spent several months living in our tent trailer at an RV park in Yuma, becoming acquainted in the course of that time with two very different segments of the local community: the Mexican American neighborhood around Eighth Avenue—La Ocho—and the "snowbirds," typically retired "Anglos" from northern US states or Canada who escaped their own winters and lived, on a budget, in the dependably warm climate of the Arizona desert. Two such different worlds, surviving in the same desert alongside one another, but rarely interacting. One day, we were driving past a "wedding chapel" in downtown Yuma on whose lawn something strange was going on. Local policemen were moving among the crowd of plainly disconcerted attendees, several of them busy grilling the groom. I pulled over and risked asking a lone policeman what was going on. He told me that they had been tipped off that the groom was in fact already married and they were there to investigate. Who, I wondered, would have made such a call? My answer, drawing on all I had learned about life in and around La Ocho, was "Love and Lettuce." The following story—"NAFTA"—was also based on an actual event recorded in a local newspaper. An RV piloted by an elderly "snowbird" couple was searched at a checkpoint when it scraped over a speed bump, sending up a shower of sparks, revealing a large cargo of migrants within. Once again, a backstory suggested itself, in this case drawing on the particular anxieties of another group of "foreigners"—the Canadians I knew from the RV parks. But the juxtaposition of the stories also suggested a way of showing the links that might tie the two communities to one another, both so defined by the larger context of desert and border. Likewise, the conflicts explored in "Endangered Species" and "Burying Sheila Cassidy" were based on my direct experience of conflicts and dramas in those places.

Beyond their genesis in the course of fieldwork, the stories are anthropological in several senses. Insofar as I have an irredeemably anthropological view of human life, nearly all my observations, views, and interests are tinged by that general sensibility. But particular anthropological topics that drew me to the region in the first place certainly guided and shaped my observations and hence animate individual stories and emerge as themes in the collection.

One of these is the power of space and place in shaping human experience. The "desert borderland" is a space produced by both nature and human society, forces imposing and inescapable. But the places that rise and fall within that space are the dynamic product of the always creative human response to those forces and draw on the historical and personal circumstances of the people that comprise them. They are wonderfully varied: from the Native American villages to the Anglo cattle ranches; from Mexican border towns offering tourist experience to US neighbors while preparing their countrymen to cross in the opposite direction to their *cuates*—nonidentical twins—on the other side (in some sense American versions of Mexico with all the contradictions that implies);

from ethnically stratified mining towns to the colorful and ephemeral youth gangs that carve out a communal life in drainage tunnels.

Within these places, the stories often treat another anthropological theme: the dynamic ambiguity and ambivalence of identity. While our identities are always a complex negotiation with ourselves and others, the provocative presence of the border as both a symbolic and a brutally "real" barrier raises the stakes. We meet an array of characters for all of whom the border itself and the act of crossing it are central, but quite different, experiences.

But why treat all this through fiction? I did not begin with a conscious decision to present my anthropological research findings in that form. Rather, while engaged in my loose and expansive ethnographic practice, I saw dramas and met characters that peeked my human and, no doubt, anthropological imagination, and succumbed to the more ancient allure of narrative, allowing myself to write stories. By their nature, stories privilege plot and character in a way that might be suspect in an ethnography, but in literature allows the author a concentrated and penetrating view of some aspect of human experience, and perhaps a wider range of readers' access to that view through an emotional and intellectual connection. Once on that path, one story literally led to another, and the idea of linking them to draw a larger picture of the region emerged. That ambition might be rooted in my anthropological perspective, but the loose weave of stories produces an admittedly fragmentary picture that is more the stuff of literature. There is no attempt to tie up disparate lives and places into a neat social scientific package. Rather the reader is taken on a ramble across a fascinating human and natural landscape wherein themes come and go, as motifs might in a piece of music, and characters appear and reappear as they do in life, playing major roles in one person's drama and minor roles in others. Ambiguity and ambivalence are no more resolved in these stories than they are in our lives.

Co. Kildare, Ireland   Lawrence J. Taylor

Acknowledgments

It is impossible to thank the countless individuals whose lives I was privileged to observe and share over years of fieldwork in the borderlands, but several whose help was critical in opening up places and people to my understanding must be named. Among them, I owe very special thanks to two *fronterizas* whose help in this project, and indeed in my border life, cannot be overestimated: Doña Claudia Proto and the late and well remembered Doña Matilde Proto, both of *Ambos Nogales*.

Other guides and facilitators include Celeste Gonzalez de Bustamante, Hector Bustamante, Mike Wilson, Rev. Robin Hoover, Sue Goodman, Roger DiRosa, Vergial Harp, Curt McCasland, Margot Bissell, Michael Lusk, Jeff Cameron, Ramona Encinas, Loida Molina, and the seasonal regulars at May's Trailer Park. In some cases I feel the privacy of individuals should not be compromised, so I can only wave a grateful hand in the direction of the US Border Patrol agents with whom I spent many hours talking or "riding along," as well as the "tunnel kids," whose nonfictional lives are the subject of another book, by that name.

The Department of Anthropology in Maynooth University has always provided a supportive environment for my eclectic efforts and I thank my colleagues there and particularly Deidre Dunne and Jacqui Mullally for their assistance at many points and many levels. David Prendergast was good enough to give some crucial help with some visual elements. I have also benefited from the reactions and observations of many students in both the US and Ireland, as well as the patient reading and critiques of many colleagues and friends in several countries. Among those, I owe a special debt of gratitude to the late Irish novelist and poet Philip Casey, who suggested and encouraged my "turn" to fiction and gave a close reading and many important suggestions to early versions of these stories. Other Irish literary friends also contributed readings and advice, including the much-lamented John McGahern, Jonathan Williams, Manchan Magan, Antony Farrell, and others at Lilliput Press. Dear Parisian friends, David Sherman and Laurie Miller read and advised, and in Arizona and Sonora, Joe Wilder, David Yetman, Tom Sheridan, Chris Szuter and Ambassador Ricardo Santana Velázquez were very helpful at many stages and Greg McNamee, Nazzer O. Méndez Robles, and Carlos G. Vélez-Ibañez contributed important suggestions and corrections to many of the stories. My work has benefited in many ways from the friendship and guidance of Ambassor Carlos Garcia de Alba and Fiona Roche. Special thanks are due to writer/educator David Hicks of Regis University for his patient reading, critiques, and general encouragement over the last several years. I also take this opportunity to thank Grace Peña Delgado, whose own contributions to a nuanced and inclusive understanding of the border region have been considerable, for her informed and generous "foreword" to these stories.

Two of these tales appeared in substantially the same form in literary magazines: "The Tunnel" in *Saranac Review* and "Ranch Rescue" in *Confrontation.* I here gratefully acknowledge these publications and the editorial support of their respective staffs—particularly *Confrontation* editor in chief, Jonna G. Semeiks. It has been a pleasure and privilege to work with my anonymous readers and the editors at Palgrave, whose great industry and enthusiasm have brought this book to life.

Finally, it is no exaggeration to say that this book would not have been possible without my wife and sometime collaborator, Maeve Hickey. She brought me to the borderlands; her work has consistently inspired my own; she was a crucial participant in the "fieldwork" that stands behind this work; she read—over and over again—every one of these stories, critiquing, editing, and making crucial suggestions; her photographs illuminate, in every sense, the words. But most of all, I thank her for her consistent faith in the project and in me.

Praise for *Tales from the Desert Borderland*

"If I were able to capture what we know to be true of the border region as well as Lawrence Taylor has done in this work, I would be famous. Taylor's men and women are Mexicans and Anglos and others at their best and worst and everything in the middle—as we all are—but Taylor has really pulled it off with care, love, affection, and respect. Bravo!"
—Carlos G. Vélez-Ibáñez, *Regents' Professor and Presidential Motorola Professor of Neighborhood Revitalization, Arizona State University, USA*

"In Taylor's *Tales from the Desert Borderland*, the U.S.-Mexico borderline exists, but everyday people and their extraordinary lives shape this engaging, stimulating and every so often humorous literary geography. From ethnographic fiction to memoir, to travelogue and creative non-fiction, and enhanced by Hickey's evocative and enigmatic photography, *Tales* crosses numerous literary boundaries, resulting in highly-nuanced portrayals of the past and present western borderlands, and which just might lead to possibilities for a more humane future of the region."
—Celeste González de Bustamante, *Associate Professor of Journalism, University of Arizona, USA*

"A prolific and creative scholar, Taylor has produced a series of articles as well as volumes that resonate with many audiences. My favorite is *Tunnel Kids*, a book I used often and to great effect in years of introductory anthropology courses. With this collection he has brought the full powers of his storytelling ability to bear on a topic he has come to know through prolonged contact and inquiry with people and place."
—Jeffrey Cole, *Dean of the Faculty and Professor of Anthropology, Connecticut College, USA*

Contents

1	Machaca	1
2	Hot Springs	13
3	Love and Lettuce	35
4	NAFTA	53
5	Endangered Species	75
6	Burying Sheila Cassidy	103
7	Ranch Rescue	131
8	The Tunnel	151

List of Figures

Fig. 1.1	Photograph by Maeve Hickey	1
Fig. 2.1	Photograph by Maeve Hickey	13
Fig. 3.1	Photograph by Maeve Hickey	35
Fig. 4.1	Photograph by Maeve Hickey	53
Fig. 5.1	Photograph by Maeve Hickey	75
Fig. 6.1	Photograph by Maeve Hickey	103
Fig. 7.1	Photograph by Maeve Hickey	131
Fig. 8.1	Photograph by Maeve Hickey	151

1

Machaca

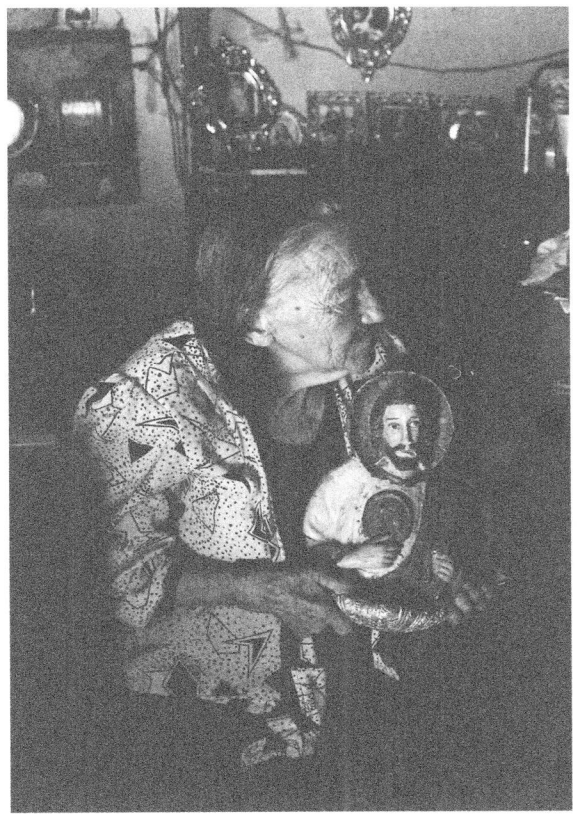

Fig. 1.1 Photograph by Maeve Hickey

Ana Rosa pulls into the gravelly yard behind *El Sueño de mi Abuelita* to find a clutch of strangers—men, women and children—waiting in the dawn shadows near the kitchen door. She is not surprised; Jimenez had texted the number "10." One of them, a young man, approaches: tentative, shy eyes surprised, comforted, disconcerted.

> *She looks like us, but different. Teeth whiter. Hair cut short with a blond streak. Will Luisa look like that in a few years, when we are all Americans?*

Ana Rosa offers only a business smile, ushering them inside through the kitchen to another door leading into the basement. They troop wordlessly down and settle themselves in among the sacks of dried beans and rice to wait.

At noon, Orozco pushes heavily through the front door of the restaurant as if performing a search warrant. Clark follows, but pauses to admire a colorful mural of life in the eponymous *"Abuelita's"* tropical village brightening the walls, padding respectfully through the dining room as if it were a path through the *pueblito michoacano*. He takes a chair opposite Orozco, who has found a seat in a dimly lit corner facing into a large mirror with a view of everything and everybody behind him. Eyes in the back of his head. Like a Goodfella at a favorite pasta palace. In Orozco's case, the gun is in plain sight, holstered beside other dangling tools of the law-enforcement trade.

"I'll take that table myself," Ana Rosa mumbles, snatching the pad from a puzzled young waitress and nodding toward the corner where the two men in uniform are leaning over their menus. "I already heard about that fat *pocho* bastard. Of all the restaurants in this fucking town, they come here? And today? *¡Que pinche vida!* Let me deal with him." Patting her already perfect coif, she sets off through the swinging door into the dining room.

Orozco has picked up the menu, his deeply lined face a battle ground between hope and disdain as he recites the names of the dishes, "*caldo de albóndigas, pozole de Jalisco, pollo estilo Michoacano,*" intoning them in his ponderous *norteño* baritone like poetry, like sacred texts. His eyes well up with longing as the words roll about his mouth. Savory memories: less delicate than a madeleine but fit to conjure the warm chatter and pungent aromas of his Tía Josefina's kitchen. Then his face darkens, like a toddler whose scoop of ice cream has tipped off the cone and landed on his shoe. If he orders any of those beautiful dishes, he will be served only disappointment.

Clark looks up at Ana Rosa, whose scarlet lips and cocoa eyes say "*bienvenidos.*" He beams warmly in reply, but she is looking at Orozco, whose big head remains buried in the opened, plastic-coated menu. He turns a page and finds a slip of paper: a hasty addition of "today's *especial.*"

"*Machaca!*"

He reads it aloud with an exaggerated Sonoran lilt, as if the word announced the Second Coming. But the eyes he fixes on Ana Rosa are hooded by a brow arched with irony. As if any place in this town could deliver on such a promise!

Ana Rosa gulps; she hadn't OK-ed that dish. But she remembers that *pedote*, Bustamante, the new chef she hired only yesterday, is a *Sonorense* from some God-forsaken hole near Hermosillo. Chef! Puebla has chefs. Michoacán, Oaxaca, La Capital, Jalisco. But the land of sand, cattle, narcos and kidnappers through which everybody must make his painful way *norte*? What have they got to cook? Stringy cattle and *tortillas de harina* are not a cuisine. Chef? A worthless *flojo* more likely. He showed up for his first day this morning an hour late, hauling a filthy sack she feared was his laundry and emptied it right onto her clean cutting counter—an avalanche of *chiles, aguacates, nopales,* and a dozen sacks of dried, shredded god-knows-what—all the time raving in what was probably a meth-induced ramble about real Sonoran food and how you couldn't get it in California, "Not everybody wants *esos chingados tacos de pescado!*"

Gripping her order pad, she risks a knowing nod at Orozco.

"*Señor Bustamante, nuestro chef, es Sonorense. Debe ser machaca autentica.*"

Authentic? Orozco is sure she's bluffing and, as if to raise the bet, orders platters for both Clark and himself. He watches closely in the mirror as Ana Rosa strides back through the swinging door into the kitchen, catching before it closes, he is sure, a worried look on her face as she turns toward the stove to repeat the order.

"That woman," he explains to Clark, "is from Michoacán. She doesn't know machaca from caca. And if there's a Sonoran in her kitchen, he's probably some *chingado mojado* who lied his way in! You watch, his *chirle machaca* is going to run over the plate like diarrhea. And his day's going to end real bad when I haul his skinny ass in!"

Orozco is cheered by the thought of any impending arrest, but having Clark there again looking up to him with that callow beach boy face, his smile deepens with nostalgia.

* * *

It was Clark's first day on the job. They were standing outside the car somewhere in a maze of empty hills by Smugglers' Gulch near the Tijuana border. Orozco handed him binoculars, nodding toward the south. Atop the next ridge they could see rows of stunted shrubs in the first gray light. But then they were moving. Swaying slightly, edging over and down the slope. Against the whitening sky the shrubs became human, branches now arms, moving steadily toward them through the high grass.

"What the hell?" Clark searched Orozco's wide, impassive face for some clue. "Is that the Mexican army coming our way?"

"Nope. That's our first group of customers."

Orozco was enjoying the moment, playing the wise, weary veteran, checking his watch and leaning back against the patrol car. Clark tried to count the figures as they disappeared into the lower ground between the ridge and themselves.

"Shouldn't we call for backup, then? There's got to be fifty or sixty of them."

"Closer to eighty, but we won't need any help. We'll wait till they reach the bottom." He motioned Clark into the car, nodding toward the radio. "Just give our coordinates and tell them to send two buses to pick them up."

When the last of the figures disappeared into the flats below them, he signaled Clark to start the engine and ease the Blazer downhill along the hard dirt road. They rolled to a stop amid the fields of dry grass, where the migrants had already sunk down into the foliage, crouching beneath view. He leaned over Clark and flipped on the high beams and the flashing red, white and blues, lighting up the field like a disco ballroom, and then hauled himself wearily from the car. Clark followed, soft and innocent even in uniform, his hand fluttering nervously over his holstered gun. But Orozco had already strolled out to the center of the field, standing, arms folded over his belly, calling out for the migrants to show themselves. They rose from the grass like extras in some B horror movie, and then moved meekly toward him, resigned to their fate.

For Orozco, Clark was at first sight a poster boy for everything wrong with the Patrol. Softly focused green eyes, harmless grin, and loose waves of streaked hair peeking out from under his cap: another good-looking, empty-headed surfer drifting through his life and the perfect San Diego seasons. There was nothing soldier about him.

Yet, there was something that drew Orozco to the boy, despite himself. Like most of his kind, Clark had crossed the border only once before, on a high school beach trip to Ensenada, during which he failed to get laid, spending the night vomiting over the edge of a red satin sofa, never fully realizing he had entered another country. But now, even though constantly embarrassed by his own clumsy ignorance, Clark was clearly entranced by the vibrant cacophony of life on the other side of the fence. Orozco watched with amusement as his partner encountered the often unexpected and sometimes poetic moments of border life. Like when the little girl in a pure white First Communion dress suddenly scampered away from her proud parents to offer him *una paleta*—frozen fruit bar—through the chain links.

Over the weeks and months, Orozco slowly dropped the jaded drill instructor act, becoming instead an increasingly enthusiastic tour guide to a world he regarded as his own. They were a comical pair, especially walking the jumping border streets. Clark: slim—though thickening a bit on border lunches, beach boy tan, green eyes shuttering like a camera in constant surprise; Orozco towering over him, unabashedly huge, strolling like the emperor through a sea of parting subjects, gray-flecked black mustache and darker eyes that saw all, even while staring unblinking ahead.

Vigilant for any chink in his nation's armor, Orozco was equally alert to cuisine, taking Clark on critical tours of every rolling *taqueria* in endless quest of the perfect *tacos de birria, de cabeza, carmelo, y al pastor*. And while they ate, Clark got Spanish lessons, Orozco laughing and making him repeat every word or phrase until he got it right.

Each meal reminded Orozco of others, the features of which he liked to recount in detail and with great affection. Especially those consumed at his *tía*'s.

"Every Sunday it was *pozole!*"

They were taking a dinner break in their car on the beach, assorted tacos soaking through the ripped-open paper bags spread between them on the seat. Just to their left, the border fence cut through the sand and continued several dozen yards into the Pacific Ocean: an emphatic statement of the prevailing moral geography. Clark had spent much of his life on such beaches, only without fences or other signs of limit or containment. Water and sand without end, or an ending.

Orozco was chewing and talking.

"See, you gotta use the right ingredients. The hominy's gotta be good of course, but it's the *chiles* that make the difference. *Guajillos.* They have to come from D.F., man—*La Capital.* The pot would simmer away there all morning when we came by, first as kids, later with our own families. And my mama and *tía* would cook together, *tamales, tostadas, rellenos … todo*, man, we fuckin' ate all day."

"Where was that? Your *tía*'s?" Clark knew that Orozco was from southern Arizona, but he was becoming increasingly sensitive to the particularity of place.

"Nogales. We call it Ambos Nogales, 'both Nogales,' because there's one on each side of the border. We were born and grew up on this side. My *Tía* Chata was on the other side. Just south of Nogales in a *ranchito* called Cibuta. That's where we would get together."

"¡Hola! ¡Hola!"

Two little boys were dangling over the water from the chain links on the Mexican side of the fence, shouting enthusiastically. When Orozco and Clark turned to watch through the windshield, they dropped into the sea with yelps of glee.

Orozco chuckled despite himself but quickly turned to one of his other favorite topics, telling Clark about a particularly clever arrest he had made, popping up behind the last man in a line that had just made its silent way in the dark of night around that very fence.

"Do you ever feel funny … I mean … does it bother you to be arresting Mexicans all the time?"

As soon as the words were out, Clark was sorry he spoke. Orozco met his young partner's hesitant look with a hard stare and then continued in a voice of patient instruction.

"*Mira*. Look. What matters is what's inside. Some guys are divided inside. Not me. I got no trouble with who I am. I am American. It's that simple. My father was a Marine. He fought in Korea and lost his brother there. And I was a Marine in Iraq. When I got home, I just put on a different uniform."

Clark nodded sheepishly, as if he hoped Orozco didn't think he dared question his loyalty to a country that Clark himself had all his life taken absolutely for granted.

"If other people have a problem with that…"

Orozco's was suddenly agitated, as if reacting to more than Clark's question.

"If they can't see a Mexican American as American, as American as any Italian, Polish, Jewish, Irish—or whatever the fuck flavor they happen to be—American, then that's their problem."

Clark was still nodding, but Orozco knew what he was thinking—none of those other American "flavors" spend their lives going back and forth on a weekly basis to the land of their grandparents, nor are they poised at the border protecting America from an inundation of their relations. Orozco, however, managed to talk himself through any possible ambivalence. After all, *his* American experience, a series of traditions from *pozole* to the Marines defined and anchored him, perhaps on the edge of America, but still in it. Clark, on the other hand, couldn't help but feel that he himself had no such anchor, no such place.

Unless it was the beach. His eyes turned again to the bisecting fence, and he gunned the patrol car into life. As Orozco buckled in, muttering about his crazy surfer partner, Clark took them bouncing over the rippled sand right at the roaring water. He spun the wheel at the last moment, and set off north along the sea edge, shooting back great arcing sprays of wet sand and water, to the noisy approval of the kids once again clambering up the fence on the other side.

Then everything changed with Operation Gatekeeper.

The Station Chief was annoyed, not with the strategy, but with the name. He would have been happier with any sports metaphor—even

Goalkeeper would have been an improvement—but he much preferred football. Football made sense and offered purpose in a way that life sometimes did not. And this stage of play called for a determined resistance that had been well captured by the name used in El Paso: Operation Hold the Line. So, he borrowed the title.

"That's right, like football." The Chief looked like a desperate coach, hunched squinting over his maps and rosters. "Doesn't matter what the quarterback is doing if the others break through."

He was right about one thing; his men weren't keeping any gate. They were on the line, and the line had been pulled wide. Two high fences of corrugated steel formed a sky-roofed tunnel through which the green and white border patrol cars could travel. But mostly they just sat crosswise, facing south, one fence ahead and another behind. Mexico was gone, replaced by featureless metal. Looking down the line at the inward-curving fence, Clark might imagine, if only for a moment, a great pipeline surf, frozen just as it broke, catching the perfect, endless wave, shooting through miles of glowing green funnel. But the image faded, and he was back in the car, enclosed between walls.

Waiting.

Orozco, always the military man, saw the logic in the new strategy.

"Think of these people living along the fence. Every day, hundreds of people charging across their yards. They had to do something, man."

That didn't make him happy with his own role in the regime. Clark watched him twitch like a caged bear in the driver's seat, his massive hand tightening on the steering wheel, his eyes scouring the fence tops as if he expected an assault that never came. No surprise when he badgered the brass into coming up with a roaming special ops detail checking shops, corners and back alleys of San Ysidro and Otay Mesa for smuggling operations.

Meanwhile, Clark remained on the line, and after another change in the system, sat alone in a car, calling in crossers. He had hoped that meeting Orozco for lunch would enliven his colorless life.

* * *

Orozco has risen from his seat to inspect the mural of "*Abuelita's*" village, eyeing every detail skeptically, as if in the hope of exposing a forgery. Clark watches him as he wanders back to their table, sinking awkwardly into his chair. Orozco isn't happy in this new assignment. Maybe it's the lack of a border in these neighborhoods—no clear line between himself and the world he now roams at will. Or maybe it's the absence of someone like Clark to guide, and in so doing find for himself the unexpected beauty of a place that now is only ugly to him, somehow an affront to his childhood. Orozco *wants* to be disappointed, though "disappointed" is not really the right word, doesn't really explain the smile, however grimace-like, that plays in the corner of his mouth. Doesn't account for the rather self-satisfied moral superiority that animates his eyes. Maybe he needs every one of San Ysidro's many Mexican lunchrooms to fail him. To keep his distance. To remind him of the imagined gulf that separates all of them from himself.

Back in the kitchen, Hugo Bustamante rips open a plastic bag of machaca he bought this morning from the desperate vaquero hawking sacks of the sun-dried shredded beef at the crossing. He tips the powdery dry contents into a sizzling skillet full of finely diced tomatoes, tomatillos, peppers and onions—moistened by oil and tears shed from eyes stung by the searing *chiltepín* he has crumbled in for good measure. Ana Rosa is watching, impressed despite herself but worrying that *los malditos migras* will smell more than lunch. She can't keep herself from looking at the door leading down into the basement. That slick *pendejo* was supposed to show up hours ago. She checks her watch and looks out the back window over the low fence to the alleyway, full of squawking kids and animals, the occasional low-rider, but no *pinche* Jimenez. She turns back to Bustamante, who is arranging the platters with due diligence and not a little artistry and decides to follow him into the dining room.

Orozco knows the lunch is coming well before he sees it, and reluctantly allows himself to believe what his nose is telling him, provoking a concatenation of images, postcards from his past—machaca in Tia Josephina's, machaca in his favorite Sonoyta café, even the machaca he made (as best he could) from dried goat meat in Iraq. He is nearly dizzy with the remembered *platillos* when the material, heavy, unfired clay platter thuds on the table before him. The clumps of singed meat look and smell perfect. Just slightly moist, a reddish brown punctuated by dots of red and green, no runny liquid, and as aromatic as a spice stand at the Guaymas market. Clark is happy to see the rapture in his partner's eyes but wonders how he will handle such a lack of disappointment.

But there's more. Orozco peels back the napkin covering a plate of tortillas and reveals a pile of neatly folded *tortillas de agua*.

"Fucking *sobaqueras*! Can't believe it."

Like a priest readying the altar cloth for Mass, Orozco lifts one with the dainty tips of his sausage fingers and lets it drop open to reveal a delightfully thin and delicately seared tortilla the size of a pizza.

"These are pure Sonora! I spent hours watching my *tía* thinning the dough on her arm, from the pit to the hand—that's why we call them *sobaqueras*. It's the lady's sweat that gives them the flavor! Then she'd cook them a few seconds on each side on a cooker made from an oil drum with a *disco de arado* on top. The discs they use on plows, to prepare the earth for the wheat, are reused to cook the tortillas. That's Mexico for you! These are the only tortillas big enough to make real burritos. But the best way to eat them is just like this…" He rips off a piece and uses it to wad up a packet of machaca to stuff into his watering mouth.

Ana Rosa is watching all this from a safe distance, but seeing Orozco's uncontained joy, she returns to the kitchen, just in time to see Jimenez's battered blue handyman van rattle through the alley gate into the yard.

"I'm gonna get them out while those two are busy eating, OK?"

She nods to Bustamante, who has been peeking into the dining room at his satisfied customers, to open the door to the yard, and shushes the *Michoacanos* as they clatter noisily up the wooden stairway from the basement. They file out and line up behind the van with their backpacks, like kids going on a school outing.

Ana Rosa is finally ready to exhale when the dining room door swings suddenly inward behind her. She spins around to find herself confronted by the hulking *migra* diner, his face as astonished as it is joyous.

"I have to meet the *cabrón* who made that machaca!"

Ana Rosa nervously backs away from him toward the door leading to the yard, in a vain attempt to block any view of the would-be Americans milling about the truck. Clark, who has followed Orozco into the kitchen, takes in the whole scene and waits breathless for his old partner to bring down the hammer on those poor bastards.

But Chef Hugo steps into the breach, rattling his cast-iron skillet on the burner where more machaca is singeing.

"*Pa'aca caballero!*" He shouts, drawing Orozco to him with a wide wave of his tattooed arm, wafting the rich odors of charring meat and chiles throughout the kitchen.

Ana Rosa is left facing Clark, following his eyes out the back door, where that slow bastard Jimenez is finally loaded up, ready to pilot his sputtering van through the gate into greater California.

But Clark has turned to watch Orozco, happy to see him leaning over the cooktop, poking a fat finger into the skillet as he settles his other great paw on Hugo Bustamante's bony shoulder. His eyes are closed, his nostrils flared, his face softened in serene recall.

2

Hot Springs

Fig. 2.1 Photograph by Maeve Hickey

© The Author(s) 2020
L. J. Taylor, *Tales from the Desert Borderland*, Palgrave Studies in Literary Anthropology, https://doi.org/10.1007/978-3-030-35133-5_2

Devil's Canyon. Easy to imagine Satan leaping among the thousand tilting towers of wind-ground stones. Warming his red ass on the shimmering white granite. Poking his trident down into the scree and rubble, scaring up snakes and scorpions, heating the water beneath till it bubbles to the surface, steaming and sulfurous. *Aguas calientes*! Hot Springs!

"You wouldn't see this on the Interstate. Worth the extra hour." Clark looks over at Stephanie, his green eyes lit up with boyish hope. She says nothing, staring straight ahead, whipping the Miata around the mountain curves. Silver blonde hair pulled back tight beneath a black band. Bare arms tense on the wheel. Even behind the Dior sunglasses, her evenly tanned face looks preoccupied.

It was only last week the Chief had called him in. Clark found him sliding his hands over the topo map of southern California, splendid with red circles and green lines, solid and dotted.

"We've got this thing sewn up this end. Your illegal knows he's licked. We're going to start floating some of you guys east a bit. His left hand moved over the map as he spoke, looking up at Clark. You know, catch the strays."

What happened to "Hold the Line?" Apparently, the Mexicans didn't get the football thing and were now playing well off the field, so we're switching metaphors—cowboying on the open range. The Chief's finger stopped on a small black mark on the map: Hot Springs.

"*Where* is it?" Stephanie had asked.

"It's kind of a resort town."

He was sure he sounded upbeat. Not desperate. Like this was an unexpected, intriguing opportunity. For both of us.

Reluctantly closing her magazine, Stephanie wondered whether he expected her to respond. What was he thinking? What was he ever thinking? But meeting Clark's irresolute eyes, she checked herself in midfrown, offering instead a nod and acquiescing smile. The kind one uses to placate a child or senile relation. But which he was inclined to take as affirmation.

Now, moving through this strange new terrain, anything seems possible. Though he is not reassured by her audibly deep breath as they leave the highway and descend into a village of dirt streets, ragged children, and half-buried truck tire fences.

They are brought to a stop by a wobbly dog that would rather die than move from the road on which, as it turns out, the rental house stands: painfully white in the afternoon sun with wizened gray shrubs, stubble lawn, and a new asphalt drive cracking away at the edges.

* * *

"Don't worry about the yard, man, *yo me encargaré*—I'll take care of it myself. *Soy Memo, Memo Ortega, para servirles.*"

The landlord, wide grin dividing a fleshy, pock-marked face, has put down his rake and steps quickly to greet them, a heavy gold chain bouncing under his half-opened work shirt with every step. He offers a meaty hand, diamond pinky ring glinting in the sun. Clark returns the hearty grasp; then Stephanie watches her fingers disappear into his fist.

"*¡Que calor!* Hotter than San Diego, *¿verdad?* Don't worry, your house is ready, he promises, waving proudly at clapboards streaked with molten globs and runs of dazzling white paint. *Tienen todo.* Ev-er-y-thing. *Afuera*, I still got a little work to do. *Es que no sabía cuándo iban a llegar.* They didn't tell me till yesterday when you were coming. *¿Hablan español?*"

Not waiting an answer, Memo continues.

"See, I got three houses. 'Who's gonna rent them?' That's what the others here say to me. Especially how they are—'*¡que ponga colores!*' No, I tell them. White. Clean. Old boards replaced. New carpets. Cabinets. And new furniture—black leather suites and light wood, *como en San Diego. Para los gringos*, excuse me, Americans. That's what I told them."

Clark winces at the word "gringo," but Stephanie is listening only to Memo's enthusiastic description of the furnishings.

"They thought I was crazy enough to think that the city people would be returning for the baths, like in the old days. No, I told them. Not for them. *La Migra, la Patrulla,* Border Patrol!"

"You're the first. There's that girl up in the trailer, but she's gonna want a real house, no? Others will come, *seguro. Aquí sus llaves*—your keys. I'll check with you later to see if you need anything."

Stephanie casts a sharp eye over the "black leather suite and light wood" furnishings—damp Naugahyde and birch-laminated chipboard.

Some pieces still sport their triple-mark-down-going-out-of-business-sale red labels. Then she looks down at the sleek stiletto heel of her café-au-lait Nine West sling-back sinking into the brown shag carpeting. Clutching the keys to the Miata like a lifeline, she tells Clark that she will see him next weekend, when he comes home.

He thought she'd stay the night, maybe two. Didn't she pack a small bag? Then, so he imagined, they would have gone back and forth over the following weekends. Until she was ready to move. They would walk together under a starry sky rarely seen on the coast. But he sees none of that in her eyes now.

"You know, you'll have the patrol car to get around in this week and I've got a lot of things to do back home. Not to mention work—I'm trying to make head buyer, and it's our biggest season coming up."

She looks up at him and tries to smile convincingly. Like they had planned it this way. All the time tightening her grip on the keys.

"Let's just see how it goes? I mean this place. This job. You don't know if you'll stay, really. Do you? It's so far from everything."

Far from the California dream that had brought her from Joliet, Indiana to San Diego. And even farther from any imagined California future.

Still panicked by the sensation of sinking into a deadly shag swamp, she plants a quick kiss on Clark's lost face and flees, feeling the asphalt beneath her feet as if it were the first solid ground. She closes her eyes for a second to savor the roar of the ignition but begins to breathe easily only somewhere on the interstate, hurtling coastward through the canyons.

Clark throws his suitcase on the sagging double mattress in the larger of the two bedrooms, paces the carpet back to the front room, and falls into the armchair. The black Naugahyde gives for a moment and then snaps back to its original position, adhering to his sweaty shirt. He reaches over and turns on the TV. Three stations of static, one so bad he can't tell whether it's in Spanish or English. No internet connection, no books, and he has forgotten to bring so much as a magazine. Lately he has read whatever Stephanie passed to him. Nothing much to unpack. He checks the kitchen—a few plastic dishes and a half-empty jar of Nescafé.

Outside, the man across the street, who has been pretending to water his plants, nods a perfunctory greeting and disappears into his house.

Clark walks the few blocks to the main street, where he finds shuttered shops and the old Spa Hotel, a vision of faded and thinly restored glory with its multi-paned windows, western castellated roof and yellowing paint flaking and fading with distance from the grandly carved, sun bleached and cracked massive front doors. They give way to a push, and he steps into an expansive, divided interior courtyard.

To one side, beyond a sign reading "Guests Only," several small pools steam under the low, heavy branches of white-flowered trees, each aqua blue concrete cauldron has a quaint, handwritten sign: *Arsenic. Radium. Sulfur.* The pools are empty, but for the nearest one, in which two murmuring women slouch in the rounded corner under a placard reading *Lithium*. A tile-top horseshoe bar takes up the other side of the courtyard. A frizzy bottle-blonde in tight white shorts and bare feet sits at the near side, her spindly, plum-nailed fingers pushing a cigarette into the air as she addresses two shadowy figures on the far side: a long-haired, lanky fellow and a plump woman, whose collection of silver bangles clatter pleasantly as she lifts and lowers her margarita. They have such an air of taken-for-granted proprietorship that Clark feels he would be entering a private space marked out by the drooping *ramada* of dead gray palm fronds. He quickly buys a beer and finds a rattan chair at an empty table between the bar and pools.

"Like a piece of venison jerky?"

The blonde at the bar has turned on her stool. She is older from the front than from behind. Kindly gray eyes squinting through the smoke. Coral lips pulled thin with a bouquet of whiskey and cigarette wrinkles at either end.

"Come on over and join us! Clark, isn't it? We know everything here. New blood! Signs of life in Hot Springs!"

Clark smiles shyly and takes his beer to the seat next to her.

"I'm Madeleine. This isn't my bar; I just act like it. There's the owner, Josep."

She indicates a small bearded man in a Hawaiian shirt leaning against the wall by the taps.

"That's Lucinda," she waves a cigarette over the bar toward the ample woman tightly packed in a flowered dress, "and that long fellow skulking beyond is Manny." At the mention of his name a flamboyant figure sporting a wide-lapelled, sagging cream silk jacket, with shoulder-length shoe-black hair and steel gray '70s sideburns, rises, saluting with his cocktail glass.

"She's the grocery, I'm the curio shop, and Manny's our weekly paper—you might say that he's the heart, mind, and soul of Hot Springs. But we're all off duty on Sunday, which, as you can see, is our day of rest and communion here in our house of worship."

Manny raises his glass again in acknowledgement of the truth of this statement and then sinks back into the shadows. His Cheshire Cat smile seems to hang in the dark as he speaks, "Welcome to Alcoholics, you-wish-they-were-Anonymous."

"Anonymity," Madeleine adds, "is hardly an option. Speaking of which, Manny's wry observations on all our sordid lives here are revealed to literally dozens of faithful readers every Monday."

Manny glides around the bar toward Clark as he speaks and waves his glass to indicate another round for everyone.

"*The Border Recorder*. Publisher, editor, photographer, and only writer. Unless I can get Madeleine to take up her gossip column again. Otherwise it's only the unadorned humdrum of smuggling, arrests, and my occasional, unpredictable, absolutely non-syndicated 'Windows on the Past.'"

"Except when new people arrive." Lucinda speaks with a light Mexican accent, fluttering a set of thickened black lashes.

"That's right," says Madeleine, "so you better let Manny take your picture and give him your story. Because otherwise he'll make it up. The people must be satisfied."

Clark, who hasn't had the opportunity to speak, picks up the fresh beer that has been sent his way and raises it in salute.

"To your health. Nice place you've got here."

"I don't know about nice," Manny answers the toast, "but it is unexpectedly interesting, Where the U.S. meets Mexico. And California, the rest of the world. You only know where you really are when you're standing at the edge."

His remarks are illustrated with sweeping martini glass gestures toward the two sides of the courtyard.

"Arsenic baths and carrot juice. Or beer, whiskey, and cigarettes. Cures for what ails you. And somehow our reticent host manages to bring it all together under one grass roof!"

Josep responds with a meek smile. Manny takes a seat next to his new audience, lifting his jacket with a flourish as he lands on the stool, as if he were a concert pianist about to perform.

"In its day, this was a stately oasis in the rocky wasteland. A destination for movie stars and countless wealthy city women. Picture the rows of ruffles on their bathing costumes rising and falling with the swell as each new arrival slips into the steaming waters … and beyond the hotel, the simple box houses of that era, each in its own patch of rocky dust. Healthful, white seasonal cottages for the cure-seeking middle classes!"

"But nothing lasts," he pauses dramatically at this point, taking a longish sip and shrugging his sharply pointed shoulders, "and as the plumbers and salesmen barged their way into the leisure classes, the taste for refinement went the way of the dodo. Spas were forsaken for beaches and the new interstate decided Hot Springs wasn't worth an exit. This grand old lady shut its doors."

His long, gaunt face grows yet longer, yet sadder. He continues, but now in the voice of calm historical detachment.

"The cottages went empty. Paint peeled, boards cracked and split, nails popped, and everything was on the verge of vanishing into bleached and rusted piles of wood and tin when the Mexicans arrived. Clapboards were secured. Windows replaced with glass or blankets. Sporadically functioning fridge placed on a porch now propped up with cinder blocks. But most of the new owners, it must be said, transformed their boxes into cheerful pastel pink or blue family homes, sensibly extended with shady *ramadas*."

"And the hotel?" Clark asks.

"A reprieve. Reopened three years ago, when our landlord appeared on the scene, ready to cater to the newer clientele. A resuscitation, you might say, of the hotel and of our sorry selves, who strut upon this anachronistic stage as if we were living history players." He looks around the bar at all his companions, and nods in the direction of the pools, whose occupants are traipsing damply off to the "Ladies."

As night falls, the courtyard, illuminated with bee lights, begins to fill with other locals, mostly men escaping the last hours of family Sundays. The jukebox has been punched into action, and Lucinda rises to dance occasionally with one or another of the young Mexican men, whose friends nudge each other as the couple step and stoop to the ever louder *musica norteña*. Madeleine and Manny disappear into a cloud of their own smoke at the far end of the bar, and Clark is greeted by and forgets dozens of men with slicked black hair and silver-buckled belts. Everyone drinks. Frosty margaritas, long vodka tonics, and icy beers carried three at a time in the waitress's plump, dusky hand.

Late in the night, after Lucinda and Madeleine have taken turns teaching him to dance the *meringue*, Clark peers through the now pleasantly distorted bar-scape to see Josep approaching, bottle in hand. He sets down a small glass with ice and pours a bright blue drink, like something that might lift grease off an engine.

"Indonesian. Used to live there."

Josep speaks like each word costs pain or money. Small and thin, he looks a vigorous sixty, muscles a series of knots that ride up and down his arms like rodents. Greek seaman's cap and small, twisted cigar. Cheeks creased lengthwise as if folded for years.

"Dutch," Manny, who has materialized by Clark's side, says, as Josep disappears into the kitchen.

"Ran away to Indonesia. Managed to get a job in a bar on some beach in Java. Got friendly with the owner, an old queer fond of native boys."

Clark pictures Sydney Greenstreet. Manny flicks his ashes and continues, "When the old man died, Josep inherited the bar. Story is he quickly married the beautiful daughter of a native pineapple grower. Presumably didn't last, though there's no word as to why, nor of how he came to be in this part of the world."

Josep comes back into the bar, followed by a slightly built young Asian man balancing a high stack of beer glasses.

"Filipino, apparently," Manny says in a low voice. "He showed up last year like he knew Josep and has been working here ever since. And Veronica—Vero—is a local. Another 'native wife.'"

Manny nods toward the waitress, who turns to face them with a warm if mildly sardonic smile. Worldly-wise at forty, eyes like blackbirds roosting on broad cheeks. Penciled arching brows. Jet hair in a loose ponytail. She moves smoothly around the inside of the bar, pulling and pouring, while Josep perches on a stool, rising occasionally to administer small doses of his strange liqueurs, each one coming with a story and the ailment specificity of a Latin saint.

In one night, Clark has sunk like a stone into their stagnant pool. Drinks come his way and he sends others around. And in the graying dawn he is ushered into his own house by Manny and Madeleine, clearly more practiced drinkers, who of course know where he lives better than he does himself.

* * *

"Welcome to Hot Springs. Sorry. Thought you knew you were on this afternoon."

For a long moment, Clark doesn't know what the woman is talking about. Perski stands before him, all discipline, waiting for him to defog.

He rubs his eyes and realizes he is wearing pajama bottoms and a soiled T-shirt. She is in uniform. Pressed and creased. Official smile set on government lips. Clark marvels once again at how the uniform manages to subvert almost any female body. There are breasts in there alright, but their size and shape are lost in khaki. As for hips and the rest, all is obscured beneath a belt decked out with gun, radio, cuffs, and half a dozen other leather-cased implements. Everything contained, though several strands of soft brown hair have escaped the band behind which all the rest is imprisoned.

An hour later they sit in the patrol car at the highest vantage point, one of a series of roller-coaster hills split by the border fence of corrugated metal—*las laminas.*

"Always quiet this time of day. Looks harmless enough, right? But wait till evening. Five-thirty, all hell breaks loose."

Doesn't seem possible. There is hardly anyone around. The village of Hot Springs shelters a few hundred souls, nearly all of them living in the blocks around Clark's house. Jacinta, the village on the other side, is just out of sight, but Clark has heard it was about the same size as its *cuate*—

fraternal twin. No *maquiladoras*—assembly plants—or *colonias* there. Just rural life continuing as it has for generations.

But Perski is right. A presage of sunset as the light empties into the low mountains to the west, leaving the granite hills to the east glowing pink and the shadows falling long and low over bare dirt hills and fence. And then figures. Just visible, like Disney ants, they skitter over the last Mexican hillside to the barbed wire fence. They are a good half a mile down the line, and by the time Clark and Perski can reach them, five have already made it safely into the rocky hills on the US side, and the two that remain have turned back to wait a more propitious moment.

"Now check behind," Perski says, nodding toward the rearview mirror.

Another small party is managing the wire fence where he and Perski had been sitting a moment before.

"So, good thing we're here!" Clark is comfortably sarcastic. But Perski's face is determined.

"Think of what it would be like if we weren't!"

* * *

Clark settles into his new routine. The days on the line are long and quiet, checking the *laminas* and in the rocky hills to the east, the few strings of barbed wire that separate the two countries. They "cut for sign"—the one skill, beyond beginning Spanish, that distinguished Border Patrol training from the other forms of enforcement—reading footprints, tread marks, even the soft brush of leafy twigs or carpet squares used to obscure those traces in the sand. Easy enough on the dirt road, but another story on the rocky uplands. Perski attempts to study even the stones there, but Clark is convinced that only an Apache could decipher any story they might tell.

Despite or perhaps because of the futility, Clark finds his job liberating. Compared to sitting in a car between fences back in San Diego, cutting for sign is a boyish pleasure, even if the quarry is rarely cornered. In San Diego he felt as closed in, as dominated, by forces above and beyond his control as any of the would-be immigrants. Here, this tenuous border and his own impotency before it are oddly comforting. That so many were apparently finding their way over it gives him a sense of possibility he hasn't felt in a long time.

Perski does not see things that way. She could sound like Duvall's *Col. Kilgore* in *Apocalypse Now*.

"'Gain, Maintain, and Expand.' That's the plan, Clark. Did you miss that memo? We concentrate our forces first in the big cities, like San Diego and El Paso, stopping the flow. When the structures are in place, we move into the 'Maintain' phase, which we can do with fewer personnel. And that allows for 'Expand,' as we push agents out into outlying areas."

"Then what?"

"Well, then we Gain and Maintain in those areas. Towns first, till we can Expand again into more remote places. It's early days here, Clark"—Perski was annoyed by his skeptical smile—"El Centro is the current Gain target. We're just holding the line here till they can expand out from there."

"Well, whoever is holding the line, or keeping the gate, is about as effective as security at a Grateful Dead concert."

"Christ, Clark, you're impossible," Perski snorts, laughing despite herself as she lifts her binoculars to inspect the landscape over the fence.

"Have you ever been to Mexico?" she asks, still looking through the lens. "I used to go there as a kid, back in Texas. My father would take me down on fishing trips. Guess he wanted a boy. It was beautiful, and the people were real nice to us. But I couldn't go now."

"Why not?"

"For one, it wouldn't be safe for me. You know, being in the Patrol."

"But that's crazy. Lots of agents go there. A good few have Mexican wives or husbands. Or are Mexicans themselves."

"I can't see that. How can you go back and forth as if … as if nothing was going on, as if this wasn't here?" Her eyes turned toward the corrugated steel biting into the hill before them.

"Fuck, Perski, we're not at war you know."

"Aren't we?"

* * *

He and Stephanie never manage to get together. The first weekend, she waits till Saturday morning to tell him that she isn't coming out, so he catches the Sunday bus on the highway. The apartment is empty, a note says she is at Jen and Andy's for dinner and that he should drop by. He sits for a moment, turning the paper over in his hand and looking out the window at the parking lot full of gleaming SUVs. His salt-spotted old Jeep is just visible in the far corner, where Stephanie has moved it. He lays her note on the glass-top coffee table and scribbles beneath it.

Got here late—early shift tomorrow. Call you. Love, C.

He opens his dresser drawers and stares down at his clothing, but in the end, takes only a blue bandanna and the keys to the Jeep.

When Stephanie cancels again the next weekend, Clark takes up Memo's suggestion and drives his jeep not west but east, through the rock desert canyons and then down into ever drier flatlands: scrubby greasewoods scattered on hard-packed, gray-white dirt stretching in all directions. Yet farther east, the land softens and then rises around him: dunes climb and fall in great waves of fine, delicate sands: rippled, crested, smoothed, and wind-whipped into fabulous hills and valleys. He pulls off the road, deflates his tires, and roars over the dunes, losing himself on the yielding sand sea.

* * *

Vero sets a cold beer and a bowl of nachos on the counter in front of Clark.

"Hey Clarky ¿cómo estas? Memo says to ask you if you need anything for your kitchen. I told him, forget it, he takes all his meals in here! Too lonely back in your place, ¿verdad? And what about your wife, or is it girlfriend? Is she ever coming back?"

He raises his eyes in a painful grin.

"*Pobrecito.*" She laughs, patting his hand. And, despite himself, he chuckles at his own pathos. She meets his laugh with one of her own, rubbing her hand up and down his arm.

"Tell Memo thanks, I have everything I need."

"And tell him I can't understand how a guy as ugly as him could have a sister as beautiful as you."

Clark reddens, surprised by his own boldness. But Vero bursts out laughing, and then, looking back at him, blushes as well.

"You should meet my other brother, Ramon. *Tan feo*. He's the ugliest one of all."

And Vero pulls up a stool and begins to regale him with stories of her childhood in *Ejido San Rafael*, a dozen tin-roofed adobes clustered between a reedy irrigation ditch, bright green fields to the south, and the great sand dunes—his playground—that flow between Baja and the other California to the north. She conjures soft orange adobe walls and tells of her childhood in a world of men: widowed father and two older brothers.

"Ramon is not only the ugliest, he's the oldest. Then comes Memo. Then me. Ramon's at home with Dad. And now one of his kids, Concha. He had a wife from the south—*una Veracruzana*—she took the girl and her brother and went back there a long time ago. But now Concha is back. And her brother, Lobo we call him, is in and out. They are both just like their mother: dark and crazy. And Concha already has a little one, Josécito."

Vero's nostalgic tone makes it seem a world well beyond reach, so that Clark is surprised when she offers to take him there the next Sunday.

"You'll love it, and my dad can make better *birria* than any old woman or man in Mexico!"

"What about *tu familia*?" she asks.

"Just me and my mother. My father left us when I was really young."

Vero looked stricken. "Poor baby."

"I don't actually remember him leaving, only that Shirley, my mom, kind of disappeared into her room and began banging away on the typewriter. Didn't see much of her for some time—turns out she was writing her 'therapeutic journal.'"

"Did that help her?" Vero is clearly stunned by the idea.

"I guess not. Because as soon as she finished that, she was on to something else. All through my childhood it was one new Life Way after another, and each one came with a whole lot of new stuff too. You know, sacred colors and objects, new clothes, new diet, and a whole new way of talking: good and evil, energy, impurity, affliction, healing. Sometimes the changes were dramatic, like when she did her Sufi thing right after a year among the Blessed Children of the 'Perfect Master.' Everything went from red to white. One day it was all bells, dangling gizmos, and framed photos of the smiling guru; next day the place was empty. Scrubbed. And she's floating around in white sheets. But a lot of the time it was harder to tell that we had moved from one philosophy to the next, like the only thing that might have changed was whether, or not, you could eat eggs. Like they might be Holy Food, or Perfect Protein, or the Innocent Victims of Rapacious Western Carnivores."

Vero nearly doubles over laughing.

Clark has not, at first, meant to be funny, but, encouraged by her reaction and seeing his life through her eyes now, he warms to the task.

"One time—he reaches for Vero's hand as he speaks, covering with a laugh—I was with the crazy, old, Italian lady who babysat me. I think my mother met her in the vegan restaurant, where they discovered they shared an aura. And so, the old lady drops me off at my house when she's supposed to, only when I get to the door it's locked. I was six, maybe, and so I circled the house and then took off into the neighborhood. Wandered around, met different people. I was having lemonade at some house at the end of the street hours later when Shirley finally shows up, all excited, back from her Buddhist Parents' Support Group, she's like, 'Oh my God! I was on the verge of a breakthrough! I was so absorbed that I forgot all about you!'"

"Holy Mother, you people are strange!"

They are both laughing.

"Like I can't get rid of even a *primo* and your mother manages to make herself single and childless! Some trick. Anyway, I wouldn't know what to do alone. I came from a big family, not just dad and the boys, but *tíos, tías, primos, primas*. I've still got *Memo El Feo* here, and I suppose all these here at the bar are like family." Her frankly affectionate eyes survey the clientele before turning back to Clark.

"But what about you? How is it for you here now? *Dígame*, what do you do when you are not here in the bar? Are you protecting our country from all those foreigners?"

"Whatever it is I'm doing here, I doubt it will be remembered as having had any impact at all, on the border or anything else for that matter. Except maybe the quality of the dirt roads we are wearing out, or your beer supply. And as for life here, I hardly ever see my neighbors. In fact, I must have landed on the only quiet street in Hot Springs."

Vero takes a quick turn around the bar to make sure everyone has what he needs and then regains her stool across from Clark, leaning on her elbow as he has seen women lean on the border fence.

"*Mira, fíjate*. You gotta understand that life has changed here and not for the better."

She is close enough to Clark that he feels himself enclosed by her perfume and entranced by a silver, flame-wrapped sacred heart of Jesus swaying from her right ear.

"Used to be real easy-going. You know? Especially the line. Everybody had relations over there and there was no real fence, no gate, no customs, no nothing. And if any *oficiales* did come round, they kinda understood that nobody was going to go all the way to Calexico to get to a cousin's or sister's house half a mile away. So, they just let us go on like before. Of course, there was some *mota* moving across, but people had to make a living, ¿*verdad?*"

Vero smiles sweetly, as if she is talking about Girl Scout cookies, taking a moment to gauge his reaction. Clark, in fact, hasn't given much thought to drugs. In San Diego, the Customs guys were right there, so the Border Patrol stuck to people. Like everyone, he has smoked some marijuana in college, and once or twice since. If he looks uncomfortable, though, it has more to do with the enveloping presence of Vero.

"Anyway, there was *no problema* until you guys in San Diego started getting tough. The more tough you made it out there, the more people came here. So, then we had new problems. *Migrantes*, most of them hicks from the south—Chiapas, Michoacan, Guerrero, Veracruz, Oaxaca— different from us. But up they came to Mexicali and then some of the *coyotes* from there started taking them over here to cross. So, that meant some income over there in Jacinta of course. Houses to stay in, food to eat. A night or two, then cross. And *drogas* too. The city boys started coming this way, sending it across by mule—animal or human. OK, so next move in the game is for your people in San Diego to start coming here to stop all this. First patrols, then the trailer. So fine, you make it a little more harder for the people to cross, so maybe they will go out into the hills and break their ankles sliding over boulders. *Las drogas* are still crossing of course, only the price is a little higher because you boys catch a load now and again. *Bueno.* But in the meantime, this little place has adjusted. However sad we are about losing our sleepy world—*aquí en Mexico, sabe la gente aprovecharse*—people get the best out of any situation. So now they move people or *drogas*, and at least sell a little food, a room for the night, and so on. And now you're here."

She fixes him with disarming, wide-open black eyes.

"And you aren't just coming in or staying out in the trailer like that girl. You're in a house right here among the rest of us. So naturally, people might be a little shy."

Vero, however, reaches over to soothe him with another pat and a warm smile.

"Hey, that's my fella you're flirting with."

Madeleine has slipped into the seat next to Clark and shoves her pack of cigarettes across the counter to him. He takes one as Vero busies herself fixing Madeleine a vodka and tonic.

"OK, Clark, give. You've been sucking up the beer and chiles here all these weeks listening to us go on about our so-called lives, and we know fuck-all about what's going on inside that good-looking beach boy head of yours." She reaches over and musses his hair. "First off, this so-called girlfriend, or whatever she is—she coming back here? You going there? Or is it over and you're up for grabs?"

* * *

"*¿Te parecen diferentes desde aquí, las dunas?* Do the dunes look different from this side?" Ramon asks, passing Clark a bottle of *Pacifico*.

It is Clark's third Sunday visit to Vero's family home in San Rafael and he is sitting once again with her brother Ramon on the front porch looking north into the same Imperial Sand Dunes he has enjoyed in his jeep.

He turns toward Ramon, thinking that Vero was right, he is in fact uglier than Memo, but in a somehow pleasing way. He is as lean as his brother is fat, stringy and gracefully long-stepping; face of stubbled red clay, features haphazard lumps thrown by an expressionist potter, and eyes, small, dark, and piercing. Ramon works the fields for his aging father, supplementing that meager income with money earned on periodic trips over the line, but, like Clark, he is given to contemplation of the ironies of the border, not three miles to their north.

"*Sí*," Clark replies and tries to explain in inadequate Spanish that from the south the dunes look more domestic, like they were part of the homes and fields.

Ramon chuckles softly, thinking that only a crazy gringo wouldn't see the difference between the irrigated fields around their houses and the great sterile mounds of white and yellow sand that rise like a wall before them. But he knows what Clark means. On the other side, so many places and things are set aside, fenced, watched, regulated. For better or worse, on this side people live with, in, and on top of everything. Over there—*pa'allá*—a great highway passes through the dunes as if they were waves on the sea, beautiful, dramatic, and distant. Of course, the desert has a way of reminding even the gringos who is boss, like when a sandstorm blows up, covering their highway, leaving blinded drivers to falter and crash. *Pa'aca*—over here—villages cozy up to the dunes, entreating their mercy, growing little patches of maize or cotton in their shadows.

"For me it's the shortest way to the USA!"

It's Concha, Ramon's brash, plump, sparkling, gold-toothed, twenty-five-year-old daughter. She speaks in English and enjoys the rhyme. She materialized that morning, back from *Algodones*, the border town twenty miles east, where legions of North American retirees—snowbirds, they call them for their seasonal migratory habits—find more doctors, dentists, optometrists, and pharmacies than anywhere in the western world. Letting them believe that she has more knowledge of both medicine and English than she does (she had worked on the names of the drugs and her few greeting phrases till they rolled effortlessly off her tongue), Concha has charmed her way into one of the pharmacies. She has been working the counter armed with a vaguely medical uniform, a seductive smile, and an adept ear that picks up more English daily. She speaks unabashedly of her deceptions and is delighted to practice her English with Clark, who is careful not to ask too many details about the lives of any of Vero's family members. He is kept busy enough just keeping track of the ever-expanding family tree as each new relation surfaces. And nobody ever refers to Clark's line of work.

But of course, Concha's remark about crossing the desert brings it back to him.

"The dunes aren't your problem. The worst that can happen to you there is that you'll be picked up and returned to San Luis, so you'll catch a ride back here. But the canal is another matter. To get to the highway, you've got to make your way over that."

"The 'All-American' Canal," Ramon remarks, looking hard at Clark. "What a sense of humor you people have! Last year, forty people died in it. Drowned. Or worse, swept into the turbines in one of the generator 'drop' stations. There was a young couple from Veracruz—newlyweds—who came through here, you remember them, Concha? They went in the night, got past the patrol OK, but when they reached the canal, the tire tube that was supposed to be there, wasn't. Maybe the patrol had taken it. They went anyway, thought they could just float across. But the woman caught her dress on something and went under and then her husband tried to save her. The next day they found them both, tangled up in the reeds with the trash."

Clark feels everyone looking at him. But they are looking at Concha. Ramon speaks.

"You're not going that way, *mi vida*"

* * *

The next Saturday, Clark drives to San Diego to pick up the rest of his belongings. Stephanie isn't there and, though she knew he was coming, has left no note. Standing at the door before leaving, he can't help noticing that the removal of his few things does not seem to affect the place one way or another. On the way back to Hot Springs he gets an uncharacteristic text from Perski inviting him to meet her at the hotel for a drink.

"So, this is where you spend so much time."

Perski has surprised him with the invitation but amazed him with her appearance. It is the first time he has seen her out of uniform. Tight jeans, white linen shirt, hair down, and her brilliant blue eyes echoed in pinwheels earrings of turquoise set in silver that gleams even in the bar's dim light. As Clark sits trying to reconcile this new vision, she takes in the scene, noting the persistent stares of the older women and the murmurs and laughs of some of the Mexican men at the far side of the bar.

"I guess they think we're a couple now," Perski says, blinking ambiguously, then so quickly changing her expression that Clark instantly doubts his own eyes.

"How well do you know the owner here, Josep, and his Mexican wife?" She leans over the table, whispering.

"Mexican," Clark thinks, "as if they were the foreigners here."

"Not well," he answers, "I mean, I see them here all the time of course, but Josep hardly ever speaks."

"What about the wife? I see she's friendly enough."

Clark follows Perski's eyes over to the bar, where Vero is busy pulling glass after glass of beer, all the time chuckling away at whatever Madeleine is telling her. She looks up and waves at Clark. He feels angry and stupid. What does she know about Vero? "Josep's wife," as he hates hearing her called.

"I know her a little. Why?"

"Drugs. The word is that she is involved with her brothers—your mysterious landlord and another on the other side. Marijuana. Since there are no Customs agents anywhere near here, sector headquarters wants us to keep an eye out."

Clark stares blankly at Perski for a moment. He thinks about Ramon's comings and goings across the border and Memo's empty rentals, with driveways in which cars appear and disappear. And, of course, the unoccupied rooms in the hotel. Then he looks over at Vero, who, meeting his eyes with a questioning smile, holds up a glass of beer, thinking that Clark is signaling for a refill. He exhales slowly, turning again to face his partner and realizing that he does not care if Vero or her brothers are bringing *mota* into the country, that he is only worried that a relentless Perski might catch them.

"I thought it might be good to come here on a Saturday night, she says, to take in the scene and maybe get everybody used to seeing us hanging out like this."

"You look good."

Clark reaches across and takes her hand, smiling wickedly, as if to say that if they are to be seen "together," she should act like it.

"I'll tell you what," he continues, "I'll keep a close eye on her."

* * *

The very next weekend Clark is back in San Rafael. He smiles to himself, remembering how he told Perski about his invitation, impressing her with his undercover abilities. But if these people are importing drugs, he thinks, looking over the blotched adobe and tin roofs, it is hard to see where the money is going. He settles down with a platter of *carne asada y refrijitos*. Vero's father, whom he still knows only as Señor Ortega, moves quietly about the porch and kitchen. Ramon sits silently, watching his fields. Concha is restless but busies herself getting beer and food for the others, her little one wobbling behind her. And Vero sits beside him, the heat from her body nearly singeing his side. The sun is low in the western sky, throwing a sharp golden light across the tops of the dunes, so that they cast three long shadows from sharply etched crests. Vero trails a finger down his back and, leaning over, brushes her lips against his neck.

"Clarky…" The whisper disappears into the evening as if it hadn't been uttered.

On the way home that evening, Vero talks of Josep, of how much he has done for her, "*y por mi familia*. Like helping my brother to come to the US, or even money for school for Concha. She's something, huh?"

Clark pulls into the dark drive behind the hotel and takes Vero in his arms, shaking with excitement.

When they have finished a long, luxurious kiss, Vero speaks.

"I want to bring her over here, Clarky. She wants a better life over here. Ramon doesn't want her to come, but in his heart, he knows she is going to go one place or another, and here is better."

* * *

Clark is awake early enough to watch the stars fade back into the lightening gray, hear the first noises of the stirring multitudes, and smell the bacon burning on the morning fires, around each of which toy-trailers or trucks are circled like frontier wagons. Thousands of feckless, sun-struck, beery Californians have gathered here in the Royal Dunes, south of the All-American Canal, for the Spring Quad Rally. Soon the rising sun illuminates their colorful, metallic steeds, tires soft for the sand, whip-pole banners fluttering in the breeze, high-spirited if hung over pilots mounted and clamoring for the start.

He pulls himself up into the jeep as the gun fires and the quads roar and splutter off up the first sand mountain. Following, he tacks crossways up the dunes with the greater skill his larger vehicle requires, and then hurtles down the other side, letting the unbraked momentum carry him up the next bank. From the top, he looks southwest, where dozens of quads are whining in a high-speed chase through a long trough, closely watched, as he knew they would be, by the two Border Patrol agents stationed there.

They stand outside their patrol car, on its shady side, with binoculars trained on the rushing metallic horde. Looking at them, it is as if he were seeing himself from the outside. A uniform, a set of tasks, the minor rebellion of pausing to watch a race. Are they sleep-walking through life? Has he been? And what was he doing now? Had he awakened? Or was he simply diverted into another waking dream?

Looking out, rather than in, Clark sees a beckoning white sea of wind-sculpted waves, eternal yet shifting, glistening in the morning sun, ignorant and uncaring of human posturing about where anything begins and ends, whether people or nations. He turns the jeep south and rolls as quietly and smoothly as he can manage down the slope and then up the next hill. There, safely out of sight and earshot, he guns the engine, spinning the wheels for a moment, then catching enough traction to send the jeep off into the air like a rocket. Bouncing to earth, he skitters over the sands for a couple of miles and then past a solitary stone marker, into Mexico.

Ramon, who has been clearing an irrigation ditch, looks up to see the jeep roll down the last dune, through the strip of scrubby wasteland, past the *tiendita*, and onto the dirt road before his house. He stands staring for a moment and then goes inside. By the time Clark has dismounted and shaken the sand off his pants, Concha has emerged wearing jeans and a baseball cap, leading her toddler by the hand and carrying a large backpack. Ramon can't make himself go farther than the doorway and watches as his daughter and grandchild climb into the jeep. Concha gives her father a brazen salute, but with an awkward finish. Clark nods toward Ramon, and rolls off toward the dunes, retracing his path through the sand sea into the US.

* * *

The next Sunday Clark is back in the courtyard bar, wondering what he will tell Perski about progress in his undercover mission. It is quiet for a moment, and then Manny and Madeleine burst in, laughing, just as Vero emerges from the kitchen proudly carrying a platter of perfectly charred *carnitas de puerco* topped by grilled scallions. She sets it grandly before Clark, and then pulls him a pint of beer.

"Concha tells me she likes it in Yuma. She sends her love."

Madeleine raises her glass from across the bar, while Manny slips into the seat next to Clark.

"You were enough to bring Madeleine out of retirement." Manny winks, shoving a folded newspaper across to him.

Clark looks down to see a mugshot of himself in uniform—no doubt drawn from the Patrol's personnel file—and a few smudgy lines of print beneath.

"Hot Springs is doubly safe now that the ever-vigilant agent Barbara Perski has been joined by San Diego native Clark Graebner. The veteran agent has made himself at home in our little community, and we are all happy to welcome him. This reporter has noted his attendance at a variety of local functions. A sociable fellow, he also enjoys, we are told, four-wheeling in the dunes. And ladies, it seems the handsome Clark just might be the most eligible bachelor in town."

3

Love and Lettuce

Fig. 3.1 Photograph by Maeve Hickey

"*Mira eso, chica* … here she comes," Concha whispers. She and Rita scrunch down in the wide front seat of Rita's Dodge Ram, draining their Thirst-Busters through purple straws and peering over the dashboard.

The golden stretch Caddy floats like a yacht down First Avenue, past colorful if modest bungalows, and eases into its gravel berth beside *White's Wedding Chapel*: a rambling Edwardian that anywhere else would be a funeral home. Here in resourceful Yuma it provides the perfect setting for the young woman avoiding both church and Las Vegas—she can picture herself arrayed in all her nuptial splendor on the well-watered lawn, a rare patch of green in this driest of desert towns, proud to be seen by all the folks on their way to a platter of *carnitas* around the corner at Jacinta's, where the big pink pig smiles above the doorway.

On this day, the ceremony will unfold in the benign glow of the soft winter sun. With the arrival of the limo, the guests find their seats in the rows of folding chairs, and the groom, his vigilant mother, and aunt upright and alert in the first row, takes his place in the flowered pergola, trying not to fidget with the rosette in his lapel. With due drama, the father of the bride, a slim, bow-legged *vaquero* in his best soft yellow ostrich boots, emerges from the limo, settles his Stetson against the breeze, and reaches back into the car. Bracing his boot heel on the curb, he holds his breath and, as if to lever a reluctant calf from a bovine womb, gives a vigorous yank. Out into the sunlight pops the mother of the bride, swathed in pink lace, wobbling on her heels as she adjusts ample rolls of flesh straining against the fabric. He reaches back into the limo to gently deliver their daughter, a fairy queen floating out on a cloud of cream satin.

Concha and Rita watch intently from the truck as the bride deftly gathers up her satin and prepares to sail down the grassy aisle to claim her prize.

"*¡Que bonita!*" Rita whispers, forgetting herself.

"*¡Puta!* Bitch!"

"*Lo siento*. Sorry. Not her. The dress…"

"Just you wait. *Esa maldita bruja*'s gonna look damn silly in that dress!" Concha pulls a cell phone from her bag and begins to punch furiously at the buttons.

* * *

Concha and Rita met the year before at the *raspado* stand on *La Ocho*, as Yuma's Eighth Street is known to its inhabitants. Concha had "crossed" a few months earlier and found a place with Lourdes, proprietress of the *Tortillería* bearing her name, who, taken with little Josécito's fondness for her *conchinitos* (little pastry pigs) and the rough charm of his mother, offered a room back behind the shop over the garage. To Concha's eyes, it was "a sweet little *apartamento*, with new lino and Formica kitchen in one corner, curtains, carpeting, a sofa that changed into a bed—*todo*!" And when a squirming Josécito was plopped down, he crawled into the corner and started grazing on the new carpet like *una vaca contenta*. He smiled up at the ladies, who burst out laughing.

"OK," Lourdes said, "you two will be fine here, and I'm gonna ask fifty dollars a week."

"*¡Que Padre!* You have a deal!"

And the deal turned out to include a job up the road at Matilde's *raspado* stand.

"You know that *puesto*—I've seen Josécito's little face streaked with mango, *¿verdad?* The girl who owns it has been saying she could use someone to work there in the evenings, and maybe weekends. I already told her about you, and she agreed that you could have the little man there with you, sleeping behind the counter while you hand out *raspados*."

So, Concha settled into life on *La Ocho*, and despite the poor quality of Matilde's *raspados*—the ice was too chunky and there was no real fruit, just syrup—she liked the whole feel of the little stand there, right away picturing herself leaning over the counter handing a big mango cone to Josécito's future father, flirting with one eye and keeping the other on her laundry across the street, for the local laundromat consisted of a long bank of outdoor washers and dryers chained to a concrete wall built into the hillside.

But the money was barely enough to live on, and as for flirting, the stand turned out to be no fountain of romance. Her customers were mostly other young mothers already dragging two or three little ones they were trying to shut up with syrupy ice. And there was Concha behind the counter sporting L'Oréal Ripe Tomato on her hungry lips. Wasted. That is until the day she decided to change the recipe. Not of the lipstick, of the *raspados*. Matilde had gone for the weekend and left Concha in charge. She shaved the ice real fine and bought a big sack of mangos off a truck by the border, cheap because they were one day too ripe to eat and perfect for *raspados*. She told her customers that if they wanted the real thing then the flavor of the day was mango, and soon the stand was surrounded by very happy patrons. Concha was thinking that if she owned the stand, she could make a fortune with it. Maybe even bring in a whole better class of *clientes*, like even a father for Josécito. She pictured a chain of pretty little stands—"Conchita's Raspados"—brightening the lives of Chicana America. But she would never make enough money working for Matilde to get even one place of her own.

That's when she met Rita, who alone among the happy customers that day appreciated Concha's lipstick. They were like lost sisters from the beginning, *cuates* of the kind that complement rather than repeat one another. Rita was as slim and pointed as her sparse conversation, with three years on this side of *La Linea* among dusty heads of lettuce—Iceberg, Romaine, Green Leaf, Red, Boston, Buttercup. Concha, the new arrival, was as round and firm as *un melón grande*. She was looking for a boyfriend; Rita was looking to get rid of hers. Seduced by her first spoonful of finely shaved ice soaked with real mango, Rita listened as Concha confessed that she was dying in that *raspado* stand—socially and financially—and determined to nag her foreman until he agreed to take Concha on at the lettuce.

* * *

"How many muscles do we got, *hermanita*, that no matter how much you work in this *pinché vida*, when you do something new, like this lettuce business, you sore all over again?"

They were limping through a cloud of smoke—pungent with charring strips of *carne asada* and bunches of *cebollitas*. The job was making her much more money than the *raspado* stand but she felt like it might kill her long before she had enough put aside for debts or dreams. She tried to stretch her cramped arms and legs till Rita, clucking softly, took a firm grip on her shoulder and began to work the knuckles of her other hand into her lower back. Concha closed her eyes, groaned, peered back over her shoulder with dismay and then broke into her famous gold-toothed smile.

"*Y madre,* this work makes me too hungry. But how can you work your ass off, and watch that same ass grow? One week of cutting lettuce from dark to dark and I'm fatter than when I came!"

Sweet winter sun on their shoulders, and Chucho's burritos—charred chunks of beef off the grill and a smoky layer of refried beans, packed into a great Sonoran tortilla. Perfection.

"Great fucking burritos, hey *hermana*? No wonder I get fat, but how come you don't, *flacita*? Or are you banging it off with that *puto* of a foreman?"

Rita pretended to be angry, pausing in mid-bite, and then deliberately lowered the dripping burrito to her paper plate. All drama, almond eyes flashing over flat, sun dark face, small mole like a hot spot between a softly broken little nose and tiny mouth.

"Chuy? His wife keeps his *huevos* in her purse, *cariña*, and the only reason I suffer his sneaky hands is to keep my *chingado* job, and yours, you ungrateful bitch! If he were still cutting lettuce, he'd slice off his own hand the way he's got his eyes always on those *nalgas* you're regretting. No, sweetheart, it's your constant nagging that's keeping me skinny!"

They laughed so hard that the men at a nearby table looked over, convinced the girls were discussing them.

"Will you look at those grinning *changos*! What a fucking selection!" Concha remarked, eyes shifting leftward to the men and then back again at Rita.

Concha paused and lifted her great sagging burrito as if it were a French delicacy, an exquisitely brittle pastry. Her plump polished fingers lightly turned the burrito toward a row of discreetly bared teeth, their even whiteness disturbed by a streak of carmine lipstick.

"I'm glad you're working with me, but I miss that *raspado* you gave me," Rita said.

"I gave you that because you scared me with that Taliban headdress!"

Concha feigned terror and then pulled her own bandana up, leaving only her eyes showing.

"And now you are wearing it too—even though yours isn't quite right." Rita leaned across the table to adjust one of the bobby pins that turned a blue bandanna into a lettuce-picker's mask.

They laughed again and rose from the table, Concha arching a painful back as she crossed the street to the lettuce field.

"It will get easier," Rita said, putting her arm through Concha's. The lettuce, I mean."

More laughter.

"But even if you have only been in this blessed country for a few weeks, you should know enough to look for Josécito's new father somewhere other than a *raspado* stand. Like move up to a *taquerilla, muchacha!*" They bent over roaring, knowing that the men from the next table were likely crossing the road right behind them.

"And another thing. That gold tooth. It's beautiful. But you need to get rid of it. If the *migra* do a sweep here, that's one sure sign of *un migrante. ¿M'entiendes, amor?*"

Concha did get used to the work. Stoop, whack, toss. And then again. And again. Soon she was moving along with the others, no longer lagging behind. Her muscles stopped aching, but what with the burritos and *raspados*—she was still working at Matilde's stand on Saturdays—she didn't lose a pound. And the job was murder on her poor hands, broken nails and chafed skin, despite the suede work gloves. So, every night she would slather on a good coat of Vaseline and sleep with thin white cotton gloves.

"You gotta stay a lady!"

Like the other women she grew to love the picker's headgear, keeping it on after work. Riding back into town, fifty wrapped heads, many topped by baseball caps, in a white school bus trailing a pair of port-o-potties, they looked like a Saudi Arabian women's softball team on tour. Then they'd fan out into the shops in small groups of arm-linked friends, inspecting gold chains in Vega's Discount Jewelry or pouring through stacks of irregular cosmetics in the 99 Cents Store. Concha drifted through the stores like the newest wife of an oil sheik, her great black, mascara-ed eyes brilliant above the mask, pulling sacks of dried pinto beans from the shelves of Food City.

Life was *suave* on *La Ocho*. Evenings, she would pop Josécito into his stroller and set out to sample *tacos, dorados, cocteles de elote, camarones y tostadas* at every sun-faded plywood or rolling tin snack shack: from *Chito's Mariscos*, with its smiling purple octopus to *El Sinolense*, Paco Molina's nostalgic tribute to his home state. She was a regular everywhere, tearing off bits of food for Josécito and herself as she kept walking west, pushing the stroller with absent-minded determination as she dreamed of possible futures. She would pass the *El Paraíso* apartments—rows of blue and white high-rent shacks with broken cars and limping dogs— and then the nicer places, with their bougainvillea-shrouded porches and raked-sand cactus gardens. To have such a home on *La Ocho* would be to have the best of Mexico and the US all at once. Finally, under the cooling gray desert dusk, she would pass the shadowy fields of cauliflower, cabbage, and lettuce, and reach the embankment on the river. There, the throbbing rhythms of *cumbia* or the plaintive ballads of the *narcotrafficantes* blurred into a syncopated hum with bird chatter and the low whirr of the river. If there were no Border Patrol around, she might walk up and listen across the narrow water to the clattering cars and people beyond the veil of reeds, in Mexico.

* * *

Saturday. Concha and Josécito at Matilde's *raspado* stand, she with a pad and pen, adding and subtracting, trying to make ten years of saving into five, or even eight, enough to buy her own modest stand. Then, with hordes of *fanático* customers, there'd be a second stand, downtown or on the South Side. From there, no limit to her expanding empire, for the Mexicano thirst for perfect *raspados* knew no bounds. Meanwhile Josécito, streaked with three or four iridescent syrups, chortled and tried with increasing success to haul himself up and out of his baby jail while Concha, with apologies, handed out Matilde's inferior *raspados*.

Concha's brother Lobo had followed her to Yuma and was also calculating his future, but in weeks, not years. He was to be seen now and again on *La Ocho*, only after dark, lurking around the edge of the *taquerillas*, listening to men with sly red eyes or boasting to open-mouthed teens. He would visit Concha to ask for money, bragging about some great deal he was just about to make. One night he turned up at the stand, looking thinner and jumpier than usual, his knowing, tough-guy smirk twitching more uneasily around his Marlboro.

He looked over his shoulder and then broke into a more boyish grin.

"Hey, *hermana, da me un raspado, a big one!* And have one yourself girl, like I just made five hundred *bolos* driving two miles down this *chingada calle*."

She didn't have to ask how. Everyone knew the system. You floated a few bales of marijuana across the narrow channel, threw them in the trunk of some shit-box car, and then drove them down the street to a local safe house. On at the end of the very street they were standing on.

"Yeah," Lobo talked fast and proud, "I just waited for the perfect moment, the change of watch for the stupid *Migra*. Then I gave the signal to my compadre, and five minutes later the weed was happy and dry and on its way home. *Que Padre!* Less than half an hour's work and I'm five hundred richer."

Concha handed him a *raspado* striped with syrups to look like the Mexican Flag—lime, white lemon, and strawberry—and divided the sum she had been considering by five hundred dollars. How many dope runs for a *raspado* stand?

* * *

Lourdes and her husband would spend all Saturday, into Sunday morning, baking. Then they slept. By nine o'clock Sunday morning, tired or not from a night at Raspados, Concha was in the *tortillería* arranging the tin trays stacked with *conchinitos*, piling the dozens of plastic bags of corn and flour tortillas, and turning on the flame beneath the giant kettle of *menudo* back in Lourdes' kitchen. Soon everybody began to arrive, sinners and saved alike passing under the green letters—*Lourdes*—and through the screen door: morning-after drunks, following the sharp scent of chillied cow's stomach and this morning's pious Mass-goers, seeking a sweet reward for having sat through another endless service. Concha was ladling a large Styrofoam cup of *menudo* by the time the first droopyassed lay-about, still duded up in Saturday night *vaquero* belt, boots, and hat, had made his painful way to the counter, his eyes straining to avoid the brilliant pink or green icing shimmering beneath the glass. Those same colors were beacons to the Mass-weary Catholics, and a few of the "Assemblies," evangelicals who had weathered even longer bouts of prayer and preaching, though broken up by livelier music and testifying.

By noon things had slowed down, and Lourdes was busy frying potatoes and *chorizo* back in the kitchen. Her son Alberto would always show up to watch the *tortillería* counter when Concha was there on Sunday, falling awkwardly into a chair by the back door, soon lost in the "Adventures of Spiderman." Rita would sometimes join them, saying little until her second cup of coffee, and then the lapses of the night before would come tumbling out in staccato phrases while Concha laughed, and Alberto pretended not to hear. Rita's sexual escapade narratives notwithstanding, Alberto preferred it when she didn't show, and he could be alone with Concha, who would busy herself flipping through a magazine, cursing softly when she failed again to score over 30 percent on a "Are you sexually satisfied?" quiz. If she looked over at Alberto once or twice, he was happy, and if she asked him whether he thought a dress was too expensive or a bathing suit too revealing for Yuma, he was shaking with quiet delight for the rest of the day.

* * *

It was on just such a Sunday morning in March that Concha met Josécito's future father. Pete Velez had been sent in for the after-Mass Sunday morning pastries by his mother, who waited with her sister in the car. The two filled the spacious back seat of the Pontiac: Tía Rosa, fat, powdered, and content, as happy as any five-year-old in the expectation of sweets; Mama Pilar edgy, her little Cantinflas mustaches twitching, head swiveling on the three layers of mole-strewn neck, awake to any approaching opportunity or enemy.

Inside the *tortillería*, Concha took no notice of Pete until she caught Alberto giving him the evil eye from his chair in the corner. She looked up and met his lazily gluttonous eyes considering her along with the pastries. Having noted his creased chinos, carefully ironed green Rugby shirt, and puffy, unworried face, she looked past him, through the screen door, at the glinting black sheen of the Pontiac, out of whose window Mama Pilar glowered.

"Try the *capirotada*, she said carving off a sample slice of the pudding cake. It's the one reason I look forward to *la Cuaresma*, Lent. But it doesn't help me be holy, *m' entiendes*, because like it tastes so good and doesn't put me in the mood to give up anything."

The tip of her tongue passed quickly over her upper lip, leaving a glistening trail for him to follow. Velez glowed, letting the *capirotada* slosh around his mouth, and then ordered a dozen *empanadas*, which Concha set daintily in a box.

"For the ride home." She smiled, sliding three *conchinitos* into a small bag and over the counter.

"It's not a long ride." He laughed, his soft face coming alive for a moment.

"*Bueno*, she said, if you don't live far away, maybe you'll come back soon. I am working here Sundays, and I live right behind."

She waved him out the front door and Alberto, tossing his comic angrily on the counter stomped out the back.

"What is your *problema*?" Concha called after him.

Lourdes was skeptical.

"That guy grew up right here in those *chingado Paraiso* apartments. The parents came up from Culiacan with a little girl, Florita. Pedro, that's what he was called back then, was born here. He was a nice boy, all right, but no spine. It was all the mother, Pilar. She sucked the air right out of his lungs. Somehow his sister was stronger, didn't so much fight back as just went along her own way. One day this *cholo* drove into town in a convertible, just cruising up and down *La Ocho* until, *de repente*, Florita was in it with him and away they went. She never came back, and Pilar never mentions her. So then naturally the mother turns everything on the son. Fierce. First thing, get him off *La Ocho*, where people like the guy in the convertible show up. So off they go to the South Side. Just a little house they got and for the same money she could have bought a real nice place here. 'Location. Location. Location.' She makes Bertie, her husband, bust his gut on two jobs to pay for it. Anyway, they keep coming to Mass on this side of town. Why? Because she wanted to be something big in front of the people over here, not something small, like her house, over there. And then one day, Bertie drops dead. I guess those jobs killed him. Pilar started coming to Mass with her poor sister, Rosa, who had moved into the little house with her. Those two women on his back, no joke, poor Pedro, or Pete, whatever—like he didn't fart without them knowing."

"But he grew up, didn't he?"

"Well, he got older and fatter. Now he is going to the community college and studying to be an accountant. Pilar tells me he is very smart. Maybe he grew up."

But Concha was already wondering when he would finish school and how much an accountant makes. She pictured little Josécito drooling on the nice green Rugby shirt and smiled dreamily to herself.

"Hey," Lourdes laughed, "my son would never forgive you, or me for putting you in Pedro's path!"

But it was on Concha's path Pete found himself wandering. In only three Sundays she succeeded in making him think they were an item, though they hadn't been farther than the *tortillería* together. Then he, or rather his mother Pilar, stopped coming to the shop after Mass. Two weeks passed and then, one Friday evening, Concha found him there when she went in to pick up Josécito. Pete stood beaming, his bland face boyish with naughty excitement, as her toddler, whom he had hoisted up on his shoulders, pounded merrily on the crown of his head. She invited him to walk, and so they did, along the edge of the darkening fields, returning to her room and his fumbling but sincere lovemaking.

And that became their custom though that late spring and sweltering summer, to meet on Fridays, stroll and dine on breaded shrimp tacos under the stars at *Chito's Mariscos*, and to grope for zippers and clasps in Concha's darkened room while Josécito slept and the swamp-cooler roared. A clumsy but heart-felt tug at her large brown nipples; a wet-mouthed kiss that just missed the sensitive spot behind her ear, an awkward roll of the hip that pinned her thigh to the sweaty sheet. But he was sweet afterward, and took easily and naturally to Josécito, bringing him small toys, sitting contentedly beside him on the rug pushing a ragged, yellow-stained little crocheted schnauzer along as Josécito attempted to bark.

In September, Pete started back to school, and Concha began to count the months to his graduation, and the beginning of their real lives together. Not that he had promised anything. They had, however, spoken at length of plans: his to open a little accounting office downtown, and hers, far more elaborate, for a *raspado* empire stretching from California to Texas, with a home office in Yuma, Arizona. But he never mentioned his mother, much less offered to bring Concha around to meet her.

* * *

In fact, college was absorbing most of Pete's attention, and not just the insoluble posers in his accounting textbook. Though she never gave him more than a glance, aloof and alluring Diana Tejera never failed to pick a seat alongside Pete. Then one day, she reached across to his desk, letting her gold charm bracelet pass softly over the long hairs on his forearm. Her long, Cinnamon Spice nail pointed to one of a series of equations.

"Do we take this one for the problem, she whispered, and put the numbers on the board in for the X and the Y?"

Pete had been sitting in a flummoxed stupor. In the dimly lit caverns of his mind, he had already forsaken accounting for his new All-Terrain Vehicle and was bouncing and sailing over the Imperial Sand Dunes when he felt the heat from her breast near his elbow.

"Right," he said, bringing himself around quickly, her perfume reaching his nose like a jolt of ammoniated spirits.

"Yeah, that's how you do it," he added, nodding knowingly.

"Thanks," she answered, a little girl smile warming a face shaped into as faithful a copy of Jennifer Lopez at the Academy Awards as her allowance could cover. One subtle gold streak accented her deep brown hair as the liner and soft lip gloss set off perfect, buttery bronze skin. She grazed his arm again, this time with three perfectly extended nails. He felt them lower down on his body though.

Diana Tejera was only nineteen. She had grown up, and still lived, in a house very like Pete's on the South Side. It was the kind of place where neighbors met while watering their lawns or palm trees, remarking on trash cans left too long on the curb. And if any housewife paused to sit outside, she did so out back, on lawn furniture. Nobody dragged her kitchen chair out the front door like on *La Ocho*. Diana had spent the last five years, while Pete was effortlessly washing out of one half-hearted endeavor after another, getting through school. And watching the older neighborhood boys, high school heroes every one of them, hit the real world like a brick wall. The few who didn't crash and burn had a plan, and so would she.

She knew that nothing was more important than looks. There she was lucky, but wise enough never to leave nature to her own devices. She watched over her changing teenage face and body as if they were a prized orchid garden, never missed an issue of *New Self Magazine and* invested every cent she could manage in the dress and make-up of the person she hoped to be. Maybe J Lo. Maybe Cameron Diaz. As for school, she did well enough in her classes to sail smoothly along, but without drawing undue attention from any idiot guidance counselor with his own designs. She flirted with every football star and class president, but never went out with any of them more than twice. She remembered her prom dress far better than her date.

And she carefully picked her best friend, Linda: light skin, thin lips, green eyes: slightly crossed. Pretty girl, but not too pretty. And presentably well behaved, at least in public. "Why don't you bring Linda along to the office with you after school?" her mother would say, having long since noted that Diana was a charming accessory in their real estate office J. Hunter and C. Tejera. Hunter had died years before, but Diana's mother saw no reason to remove a name that added "balance" to the title. "Don't want people to think we serve only Mexicans!"

Connie Tejera had been a dark beauty herself, charming her husband off a horse, and clients into houses more expensive than they could afford. Lately she had begun draping her expanding body in flowing kaftans, relying on striking silk scarves for flair, but she still managed to move real estate. As for the husband, he preferred to spend his time chasing calves over the forty acres of weeds his family held out beyond the airport. Diana was happy to hang out at the office, and her friend Linda would look up from *Your Prom* magazine to watch bemused as her friend jumped up to help clients. By sixteen Diana was as slick as a brochure, able to describe any windowless Unabomber-sized shack as a "cute fixer-upper with unlimited potential," any of 233 identical "Santa Fe's" as an "executive home."

Diana headed for the local Community College without hesitation, giving herself two years to gather a few tradable skills and a husband. She soon discovered, however, that while she felt she had already crossed the Rubicon into adulthood when her prom corsage had wilted in the fridge, the boys were still very much boys: far happier drinking themselves sick in each other's company and drifting through their classes as if they were still in high school. Not Diana. Although she moved among them with the same distracting sway, she wore the clothes of an ever-improving imagined future and started buying her cosmetics at Dillard's in the mall rather than at Walgreen's. She treated her selection of college courses with the same sense of purpose, which is how she found herself in accounting, and sitting alongside Velez.

He was just what she was looking for: seven years older, no Ricky Martin, but nice-looking enough. Vulnerable, adrift, but not defeated. Moldable. She knew him to be the child of the striving Pilar Velez, a frequent window-shopper in her parents' office. He was shy, but her opening was clear: he would make it through the course only with her help. Of course, he would make a rotten accountant. So what? She'd be taking care of the books when they took over her parents' business and until then he could use that guileless face to sell houses and run for city council. Diana figured that anyone with the right looks, an inoffensive and affable manner, and a few credentials could make a decent run. Add determination—and that she would supply—and he had a better than even chance.

As for handling the ever-vigilant Señora Velez, that was easy. Diana waited a couple of Saturdays until the old woman turned up at the real estate office, feigning an interest in the new development of patio homes out by the airport, aimed at snowbirds tired of the annual flight to and from British Columbia or Oregon. Diana, who offered to show her the brochures, took the opportunity to mention how lucky she was to have met Pete, to have so bright and nice a man as her son helping her with the class.

Pilar gave her a piercing appraisal, beady black eyes burning in a tower of folded flesh, like an obese, featherless eagle.

"Yes, he has helped me enough that I am doing well now. Of course, we have only chatted a little about other things, but he's always bragging about your *tamales!*"

She laughed disarmingly, and the old lady smiled despite herself, two of her three neck rolls relaxing their taut grip on her head.

Diana continued, "My mother tried to teach me to make them when I was a little girl, but I was too young and foolish to listen, and now she's too fed up with me to try again."

She touched the old lady's arm for a second, causing her heavy flesh to quiver. Before she could stop herself, Pilar had invited her to come over that very evening.

Diana had no trouble appearing to be a quick learner—she had been deftly stuffing and wrapping *tamales* since she was five years old—and was happy to give all the credit to her new-found teachers. And so, pressed against their young protégé and around the steaming kettle jammed with layers of their perfect, corn-husk-wrapper-twisted-and-tied *tamales*, the old sisters came as close to a joyful camaraderie as they ever had. Pete watched from the dining table, bent over an impenetrable accounting problem that Diana had worked out hours before while she applied the right soft coral lipstick for the evening. He looked up at the scene, and felt, not for the first time, that he was playing only a minor role in the story of his own life.

That week Diana was careful not to pay Pete too much attention, avoiding him in the hallways so that he would look forward to her presence three times a week in the class they shared. The last of those was Friday afternoon and she could sense his edginess. Putting that together with dark hints from the mother, she knew that the time had come to up the ante. As they walked out of class together, she told him that she had something of a date that night.

"I think he's getting serious, you know, and I…"

She let her voice trail off and turned to face him with a thoroughly enigmatic look, then kissed him softly on the lips and began to walk slowly away. He caught up with her and, without thinking, proposed that she get out of her date and instead go with him for a drive.

And so, they did (the hour of his usual visit with Concha came and went and she finally took up Rita's long-standing offer of a movie). Parked by the little airport to watch the orange blaze sunset, Diana prattled tearfully, revealing the heartaches that beset the life of a beautiful girl. She kissed Pete's hand as it smoothed the tears from her cheek and then let his mouth close over her slightly parted lips.

Pilar, who had been suffering in silence through the summer, had, of course, known all about Concha, and nearly gagged on the powerful scent of "Wet n' Wild" every Saturday morning, as she stuffed her son's clothes angrily into the washer. It was with elation and the heady sweet taste of imminent revenge that she noticed the change on that Saturday—the sly smiles and touches—when once again Diana came by for *tamale*-making.

"Why not come to Mass with us tomorrow, dear," she offered, "over at Saint Anthony's?"

Pilar smiled all the way through the appallingly dull service in happy anticipation, and then, when everyone was comfortably arranged in the Pontiac, she asked Pete to drive to *Lourdes'* for pastries.

"Diana, darling, why don't you go in with Pete and pick out whatever you like?"

She sent her out like a smart bomb and settled back to await the blast.

Naturally, Diana feigned innocence. While Concha, after a pause of thinly masked fury, began to shovel cinnamon-dusted cookies into the only soiled box she could find, Diana broke off a piece of the bright green pastry she was munching and offered it to Josécito. Delighted and disloyal, he jammed the treat into his mouth as he tried to climb Pete's leg. Pete, of course, meant to stay behind for a moment, to explain—he knew not what or how—but he let himself be led out by Diana, leaving Concha to explode into expletives as he drove away, her bellowed *pinches* and *chigadas* bringing Lourdes running out of the kitchen and sending Josécito, who was already crying for the loss of his favorite playmate, into an ear-shattering bawl.

In the weeks that followed, Concha took out her anger mainly on the lettuce, whacking unmercifully stalk after stalk. The human aspect of iceberg assisted the fantasy—at the end of the row her basket overflowed with the massacred green heads of Pete Velez. Rita was still by her side, executing her own lost loves. They took turns shouting out the names of their victims until they collapsed laughing, loud enough that the foreman turned to scowl, sure they were discussing his masculine deficiencies.

The wedding announcement came as no surprise, but that didn't make it any easier. She didn't really miss Pete but couldn't tear her eyes away from the photo of Diana in the local paper, from her look of sweet victory. *Puta.*

"I thought you had put him behind you, girl!" Rita said, wary of the fury in her friend's eyes, but more so by the serene smile that suddenly stole like a possessing spirit across her face.

* * *

And so, on the appointed day the girls are stationed in Rita's truck across from the Wedding Chapel. Rita watches in stunned admiration as Concha punches the numbers on her cell phone.

Her first call is to the local police, to whom she introduces herself as the estranged, but not-yet-divorced, spouse of one Peter Velez, who was about to marry again and, as she repeats in more detail in her second call, to the *Migra*, to an illegal bitch, whose entire family has snuck across the border to take part.

"You better get here fast," she advises both branches of local law enforcement.

Soon, blue and green uniforms are swarming through the reeling wedding party. Poor Señora Velez looks on in confused horror as her son seeks in vain to convince a policeman that he needs no proof of divorce since he has never been married, while a few yards away agents have corralled the Tejeras, who fumble through pockets and purses for evidence of citizenship. The sun begins to set, bathing California, Arizona, and Mexico in a perfect pink haze and the guests, who have wandered about like movie extras waiting for direction, finally disperse. The bride, too stunned to cry, a macabre effigy of herself grasping the gathered skirts of her gown, stands alone on the lawn but for the little ring-bearer Anthony, who busies himself unraveling the fine lace at the end of her bridal train.

4

NAFTA

Fig. 4.1 Photograph by Maeve Hickey

I

Silver Supper Night at Grumpy's and a room full of seniors are bobbing over their burgers like happy bulldogs. Ned, too nervous to eat, catches his own pallid reflection in the mirrored wall next to their booth. His face is drawn so tight it seems ready to fold in on itself. But his eyes, if watery and red-rimmed, seem younger than usual. Lit up, if only by anxiety. The Mexican—what's his name—Lolo? Loco?—is talking, the twitching smile on his pinched face seems as heart-felt as the current-induced kick of a dead frog. But Ruby is nodding happily, as if it all made perfect sense. As if they, who had successfully managed to reach their golden years without incident, were naturals for the roles of Bonnie and Clyde.

Ned feels himself rising from the table with the others.

"Thanks. Gra-ci-as, Lobo."

Was that Ruby's voice?

"Bueno, everything's set. See you in Mexico!"

Outside, the cool evening air slaps Ned back to his senses. He knows where he is, but not how he got there.

Maybe that ice storm had been an omen.

II

They had closed their home as always. Ruby wrapped and stored the glassware and crockery that she would unwrap and rewash on their return. Ned hosed down the barn, brought his few cows over to the neighbor, screwed down the windows, and covered them with fitted squares of plywood. Last, he set the bathroom faucet on a slow drip to keep the water crawling through the pipes all winter.

"That will keep 'em from freezing, eh?" he told Ruby, as though for the first time.

They liked to say that they had the best of both worlds, enjoying the sweet spring, glorious summer, and bracing autumn of Alberta, all followed by a perfect Arizona winter. But by late November the "bracing autumn" sky was thickening into an icy blanket, snow was already crusting on the ground, and frigid winds were humming between sheets of aluminum siding. Their departure often had the character of a narrow escape. And when they returned on the first of March—the three months Ned figured their meagre resources allowed—Yuma's wonderful spring was still in full force, its merciless summer still a month, even two, away, and the Alberta mountain winter would be railing on till late April.

So, the ice storm on the first of December was hardly out of season. The day began mildly enough, and the rig had been whirring happily along for hours when an angry wind rose out of nowhere, sending towering anvil clouds that blackened the sky into an early dusk. Soon Ned was leaning over the wheel, searching into a rain-streaked blackness where sky and road disappeared into one another. He spoke, trying not to look over at Ruby.

"This truck can handle anything."

But Ruby kept twisting her head to look anxiously behind, watching the trailer sway on the slickening asphalt, so he relented and turned off the highway in Dillon, Montana. First day out and exactly four hours earlier than their planned stop in Pocatello, Idaho.

"No parks listed in either Sam's Club or KOA," Ruby reported, checking her directories.

"Don't need one."

He pulled onto a grassy margin along a forest road, easing forward till the entire rig was nestled safely in the muddy weeds. The shadowy forms of low trees gathered about them in the inky night like lost souls seeking a way out of the relentless storm. The trailer was an icebox, and they huddled in the queen bed, letting the gas heater blow a blanket of hot air over them, listening to volleys of half-frozen ice pellets skitter and thud against the tin.

Ned awoke at dawn to find Ruby standing in her quilted bathrobe, staring out the window into the thin morning light.

"An orchard, that's where we are. Not a forest … an orchard."

They stood together, looking out at hundreds of apple trees, fruitless, leafless, but each one perfectly sheathed in thin clear ice, every branch and twig. As they watched, the rising sun set it all ablaze with light as if someone had thrown a switch. And though the trees were undoubtedly beautiful, Ruby found them somehow inscrutably sad, their barren twisted limbs clawing and scratching hungrily at the thin air. In a clearing among them, half a dozen forlorn shacks huddled, as if against the weather, emptied of life, their windows boarded up like the home Ned and Ruby had left behind.

"Farm workers. Probably Mexicans. Up for the apples, gone back south for whatever. Maybe lettuce in Yuma," Ned mused.

Ruby tried to picture curtains behind the boarded-up windows, and then got busy fixing bowls of instant oatmeal, followed by mugs of milky tea. She watched the ice vanishing under the climbing sun while Ned studied his well-worn trip map with dismay. The four thick red pen lines represented each day's allotted travel, the four circled towns were home to trailer parks for those nights. Ned wondered aloud whether he should circle the orchard near Dillon. But the larger issue was the rest of the trip; the few hours lost like that on their first day out had thrown them badly off schedule.

"We always meet Sid and Verna in Toby's Place," Ruby reminded him.

Trailer parks often had personal names like that, or else somebody's idea of a clever pun, like *Belly Acres*. These titles probably long preceded the reality, each conceived in desperate daydream while the author slogged away behind some demeaning desk, stamping machine, or store counter. And now, dreams incarnate, the names enlivened the pages of campground guidebooks. You can picture each proud owner: fifty-gallon shorts and a crushable all-weather hat, round-bellied, cola-toting, pacing his or her little empire or watching it through the home/office trailer window.

On to Toby's Place it was then, driving farther and faster than planned, giving Ned the chance to demonstrate—as he edged over the speed limit even in vigilant Idaho—the utility of the "cop catcher" radio unit he had purchased at a trailer park yard sale. Back on schedule, they arrived three days later at Mary's Rest in Yuma at their usual time, managing brief reunions with their favorite road warriors along the way.

* * *

Surrounded by helpful neighbors, Ned and Ruby set into practiced motion like a pair of antique wind-up toys, backing in and hooking up, she unpacking her glassware and arranging the kitchen, he setting up his birdhouses and whirligigs. With everything in place, they strolled across the park to check up on Lyle and Didi in their *Alpenlite*. Ruby found Didi inside, putting out the latest photographs of the grandchildren. Lyle was, as usual, luxuriating under the aluminum awning already draped with strings of Christmas lights, holding court.

"Pull up a seat, Ned," Lyle invited.

He fell heavily into an empty lawn chair and greeted his compatriots, "Another season, eh?"

Harold, a smug, small success in the lumber industry, slumped back into his chair, eyes obscured by hefty black plastic frame glasses and brows knitted into a great jutting ridge shading a self-satisfied frown. Herbie, recently and reluctantly retired at only fifty-eight years old from farm equipment sales, turned his small, polished white head away and fretted. But Lyle's simple, homey welcoming smile never left his farmer's face. Those sixty-some years of wheat, hay, and livestock could be read in his thick calves, massive mitts, and ropy forearms: the kind of body that said "tractor pull," except for the mid-section, which said "beer and blueberry pie" and needed all the power in his short, thick legs just to hoist it up and move it about.

There was nothing obvious to distinguish these men from the Americans all around them: same wives, trailers, burnt-wood name plaques, plastic cacti, and holiday lights. But their Canadian-ness held them apart and together. And if, as often as not, they annoyed the hell out of one another, each felt naturally obliged to befriend and sustain their fellow citizens in shared exile. And they did suffer these days from one great disadvantage. They paid their way with Canadian dollars, whose value seemed to drop every time they opened the newspaper.

"How was the trip down?" Harold asked, smirking and rubbing a thin tissue over his glasses.

No question more predictable. Harold kept a permanent "park model" and car at Mary's Rest and flew back and forth between their two homes. Edie had insisted they abandon the road and Harold, wishing to relive the adventures while reassuring himself that he was better off without them, hungered for tales of travel disaster. Although Ned would always present the journey in as positive a light as he could manage, Harold would affect dismay at the slightest setback, shaking his head with pity. Naturally, Ned found this very irritating, but since he couldn't make himself omit the slightest detail in any account, he felt that he had no choice but to tell the story of the ice storm and delay. Of course, he stressed his own competent reassertion of order.

"By the second night we were running ahead of schedule, made it to the park with time to spare for all-you-can-eat buffet at the Tinsley Denny's."

Harold groaned. "You can have it! Smartest thing I ever did, keeping the trailer down here. Flying costs a little more, but we gain eight days. We used to waste that time on the road; now we spend it down here avoiding the winter!"

"Well, we're here now, eh!"

Ned spoke with only a trace of annoyance, exchanging a quick conspiratorial look with Lyle. These confrontations with Harold always made them feel a bit younger, like reckless kids still on the road.

They all settled into the season with the usual sense of calculated fun. Yard sales; Tuesday night bingo; Darts on Wednesday. Saturday night was big: early bird special at Señor Gordo's followed by Ladies' Choice Dance at the Baptist Church. If they crossed the border to Algodones, they could get a *Sinor haircut $1.50*, visit doctors, dentists, fill prescriptions, lunch for the adventurous, digested while waiting to cross in a line of cars backed up half a mile along the riverbank. And there were the special events like iceberg bowling during Yuma's fabled February "Lettuce Days."

Not that they spent every moment frivolously. The women baked and knitted, sometimes sending slippers and sweaters to ungrateful kids and grandkids, but more often buying from each other, thus producing a profit for one lady and a bargain for another. The men washed and rewashed their trailers and cars. And clipped coupons, delighted that Food City was accepting, along with its own, those of any competitor.

Lyle had brought a new toy this season: a screw-vice nutcracker, the size of a small sewing machine, set proudly on a card table under the awning so that they could take turns popping shells, working their ways through sacks of walnuts the cost of which they had shared. Ned figured aloud that they were saving seventy-five cents a pound.

"We'd be sitting here talking anyway, eh?"

It was like Harold to choose just such a moment, when the others were happily counting nuts and the money in their pockets, to remind them that the global economy was busy hurtling along its own path, taking them all along for the ride.

"Down to fifty-eight cents today."

Harold took a perverse pleasure in following the Canadian dollar's decline.

"Fifty-eight cents," he repeated.

There was something about dropping below sixty cents. It was as if their dollar, swept along through the punishing rapids these many months, had now breached Niagara Falls and would plummet to its infinitesimal conclusion.

Herbie stared into a thirty-year future bereft of Friday night fish fries and the occasional Molson's. Lyle, rarely ruffled, grimaced as he rolled a walnut between his hands. Ned calculated, reaching the easy conclusion that he and Ruby were living well beyond their means. They had to cut back on nearly everything or else they would be facing a lot more Canadian winters.

* * *

Ruby and Didi were determined early morning walkers. Hair jammed under baseball caps, they strode past trailer parks and lettuce fields, checking for yard sales on the way. One morning, Ruby didn't turn at their usual corner. With Didi scrambling after, she continued her hip-jolting stride into Eighth Street until she found herself arrested by the pungent aroma of *menudo* wafting out from a gaily decorated adobe shop just up the block. Didi, confused by the sudden change in route, took a wide-eyed look around her, to the amusement of the stream of customers on their way into and out of *Lourdes' Tortillería*.

"All Mexicans here," Didi noted, as if Mexico itself did not begin at the end of the street.

One of the customers was smiling and waving at Ruby, holding up a bag of large flour tortillas. Ruby waved back.

"So that's where she gets them."

"Gets what? Do you know her?"

Didi looked from Ruby to the other woman, who stood smiling uncertainly in an old-fashioned print dress, still on her side of the street.

"Tacos. Or whatever they call them. You know, only they're bigger and softer around here, I guess. She goes to my church—the Assembly—and tries to talk to me in English. Tells me about the food she makes. One Sunday morning, I found a bag of those tacos hanging from our doorknob. I had no idea what to do with them and Ned said we didn't know if they were raw or cooked. They looked raw to him, he said. So, we just left them on top of the fridge until they got blue spots. Of course, I didn't tell her that I had to throw them away, but I was afraid to say we liked them either, or God knows what else would show up on our doorstep! We better go over and say hello, though," Ruby concluded with Christian determination.

Although she had finished with her shopping, the Mexican lady happily ushered Didi and Ruby back into *Lourdes'*, feeling obliged to play tour guide in the event of such a rare opportunity. Didi grew vertiginous in the sensory swirl. Color: some of the pastries were as bright as their shorts. Noise: booming local voices competing with the brass Sinaloa band blaring over Radio Frontera. And smells: a heady mix of sweet hot pastries, bubbling, chilied *menudo* and tortillas, both corn and flour, heap after staggering heap brought in on trays shouldered by Lourdes' happily sweating husband.

"*Una amiga de mi iglesia*," the lady explained, guiding Ruby by the elbow up to the counter to meet the owner. Smiling like the morning sun, Lourdes reached over with her left hand—the right was busy dropping pastries into a paper bag—and peeled a small, beautifully singed *tortilla de harina* from the top of the newest pile. "*Una gordita*," she said, rolling and then popping it into Ruby's mouth, whose surprised gape Lourdes might have taken for hunger. Didi backed out the door, grinning tightly all the way, while Ruby, now chewing away on the savory tortilla with stunned and undisguised relish, found a sack of them pressed into her hand by a proud Lourdes.

"No charge, *¡que regresen ustedes!*"

By lunchtime the tortillas had cooled and were less flavorful, so Ruby gave them a minute in the microwave before serving three to her astonished husband, each dripping with melting pads of "Almost Butter."

"Got them over at Eighth Street. They've got a lot of pastries too, much cheaper than the American bakery, and they've even got a half-price rack."

Ned looked up with interest and agreed to stop in on the way to the supermarket. They revisited the shop that Sunday after church, and Ned was delighted with his huge sack of imperceptibly stale *palmitas*, *conchinitos*, and god knows what else, all for just under three dollars. They even met some locals, including *Lobo*, a young man with an ingratiating smile and a surprising proposition.

III

"Ned, are you OK? I can drive, if you want."

His left hand is compulsively tapping the steering wheel and his eyes twitch from road to the mirrors every few seconds, yet he keeps letting the truck drift an inch or two over the ragged edge of the road, causing the trailer to pitch and jerk behind them.

They are on Carretera 2, a two-lane highway running east-west along the Mexican side of the border, the only route from Tijuana to the rest of Mexico: the inevitable daily path of thousands of vehicles. They include dozens of buses: from sleek new rolling salons, their passengers reclining behind velvet curtains watching videos, to thrice-recycled US school buses now lurid green, their windows obscured with destinations scrawled in white paint. And trucks: gleaming aluminum boxes the size of fallen skyscrapers rocketing along on eighteen wheels, and rickety farm wagons with loose bales of hay or rotting crates of fruit stacked up and over the cab, feeling their faltering way around the curves like half-blind old men. While most of these vehicles are driven by sober men on their habitual way home, some appear to be piloted by tequila- or meth-powered desperados: the kind of men whose living depends on arriving sooner rather than safer, and who take a warning sign as a personal challenge to their masculinity. In the fifty minutes since they crossed the border at San Luis, Ned has rediscovered religion. Each blind bend seems very possibly the scene of their last moment on earth, more so as the evening sky darkens, and they skirt the volcanic wilderness of the *Pinacate*, where the road climbs and curves with more frequency, and oncoming headlights are just as likely to appear in your lane as in the other.

"Lobo never said the road would be this bad," Ruby says.

Ned tightens his grip on the wheel, fighting the urge to close his eyes like a kid on his first roller-coaster ride.

"I bet Lobo left out a lot," he says. "It's not too late to pull out. We could always give back the money."

His tone says he is hoping that she will want to do just that.

"Well, we're almost to the place—Los Vid-something. We might as well go that far and see what things look like, see if he's there. Then we can decide whether to keep going or not."

Ned looks over at her, as if to say that, having gone that far, they will find it hard to withdraw. After more than forty years of marriage, they don't need an interpreter.

Ruby has been in forward motion from their first meeting with Lobo at Lourdes' until the final session at San Luis, when he pushed an envelope with twelve thousand five hundred American dollars into her trembling hand. They had gone home unable to say a word, Ned sinking into his chair on the patio, his eyes clouded and drifting. But she, energized by the thought of all that money there and more to come after, had swung into action, yanking open every cupboard and drawer in the trailer, methodically wrapping and packing. Make your trailer as light as you can, Lobo said. Then she leaned out the door and suggested that they rip out the cabinets. Ned had looked up in silent, stunned confusion.

"You know," she rattled on with inspired clarity, "lighten the load, and make space. Plus, we can tell the others that we're going to Mexico to have the trailer refitted. They're bound to be very curious about us packing and leaving a month early!"

Remembering those preparations, Ruby is reassured. And proud. She looks over at Ned again, who, suddenly smaller and frailer, is downshifting, easing the truck and trailer into the trash-strewn parking lot of *Café Los Vidrios*.

It's not the sort of place they think of as Mexican. No gaily painted tiles, smiling waiters offering English menus and dollar prices. There is, in fact, no menu at all. A young man, clearly surprised, moves uncertainly toward them over the worn linoleum floor through a cavernous, green cement room. The place smells of gasoline and bad coffee; the only decoration is a large framed map of Sonora, on which *Los Vidrios*, which seems to consist only of the café, is marked as if a large city, perched on a heavy black line, above which is written "E.U.," *Estados Unidos*. The United States.

"Dos coffees, please." Ruby holds up two fingers and then points at the map, smiling.

"Is the US real close? The border?"

"*Sí, señora*, just there."

The waiter points out the window.

"That's the US? Do people cross over there?"

The waiter nods shyly and retreats to fill the order.

They sip boiling hot Nescafé and wait, Ruby trying to distract Ned by recalling how Harold, dying of curiosity, watched them haul away the old cupboards and store their belongings.

"An adventure in Mexico? Remember, that's what we had told him. An adventure in Mexico? He just kept repeating it, like a phrase in another language."

Ned manages a weak smile.

"And I hated to lie to Lyle and Didi. Guess they never really believed us. You think they'd come in with us, if we did it again?"

Ned looks up in dismay when Ruby mentions the possibility of future runs, but just then the door swings open and Lobo enters, baseball cap low over his eyes, scanning the shadows. Ruby waves, as she would to a friend coming into a dark theater. He smiles and ushers in his clients: a stream of small bodies and dark faces, eyes bright with hope and fear. Mostly men, some women, and a few children, and nearly all outfitted in jeans, baseball caps, and black backpacks. By the time Lobo reaches their table, he knows that Ned has them counted.

"*Yo se*. More than we said. *Diez más, triente cinco*. Don't worry. You got ten grand more coming on the other end—that's twenty-two thousand five hundred. With what you've already got, that's thirty-five thousand *bolos*, amigo. But it's your choice. We can leave ten of them here if you want."

It's Ruby who answers.

"We can do it. Good thing we got rid of those cabinets!"

* * *

Half an hour later they are on the road, with thirty-five *Oaxaqueños* nestled in every available corner of the trailer, following Lobo, who, armed with a legal frontier pass, drives his own pickup east toward the Sonoyta crossing, where Carretera 2 meets 8, the road from the coastal resort of Puerto Peñasco, or Rocky Point, as it is known to the thousands of Arizonans who help the locals litter the beaches and soak up the beer. Sunday evening means hundreds of trailers choking the border gate into the US. A pain in the ass, as Lobo explained, but the least chance of a search.

"Once in a while, they poke their noses into a trailer, but not people like you guys, and no way when they got a line stretching forever." Ned repeats the assurance to himself as they begin to drive the forty straight, smooth miles to the gate.

But suddenly, Lobo, who is nearly half a mile ahead, slows to a stop at a big red *Alto* sign. A man emerges from what they could see was a guard box. He looks like the ones back in the trailer but dressed in fatigues and carrying an automatic rifle nearly as big as he is.

"Stop," Ruby says, calm but urgent.

Ned obeys, pulling over to let other cars pass. He turns to Ruby to await instruction.

She watches with Ned's binoculars as a bus is made to stop at the checkpoint and all its passengers taken off and lined up. Several soldiers, looking like small boys, pass up and down in front of them, weapons slung at the ready.

"Another thing Lobo forgot to mention," Ned whispers, taking his turn with the glasses. "Army checkpoint of some kind. But what are they looking for?"

As they watch, the soldiers swarm around several more vehicles, popping trunks, holding flashlights in windows, ordering people out onto the roadside.

"Turn around, Ned."

His head shaking, Ned sighs with what Ruby recognizes as relief and turns the vehicle around. But when they reach *Los Vidrios* again, she directs him back into the parking lot and, saying she'll be right back, strides into the café with a lively and undefeated step. She re-emerges with the waiter, who points into the dark, past the cluster of wrecked cars, to what Ned can now see is a large opening in the barbed wire fence not fifty feet behind the café.

"Remember, the waiter told us the border's close, it's right there!"

Ruby is leaning into the window, grinning up at Ned.

"José here says all we have to do is go through that opening and follow the gravel road north. Just keep going and eventually it forks, one road goes toward Ajo and the other north to the Interstate. What do you say?"

As Ned stares at Ruby, trying desperately to find the woman he has been married to, a voice makes his head swivel toward the passenger side, where a young boy has opened the door and climbed in.

"They want to know why we come back?"

"Couldn't go through." Ned explained. "Army, stopping everyone."

"Mexican army?"

"Uh huh."

"*Dinero*. No pay them?"

"Tell them not to worry"—Ruby has come around to the passenger side—"we are going across another way. A better way. No Mexican Army and no US Army, Customs, or Border Patrol."

The boy nods with enthusiasm and skips back to the trailer.

"Have you lost your mind?" Ned has finally found his tongue. "You're going to take us into the desert on the word of a waiter. How did you speak to him anyway?"

"He has a lot of English. Spent years up in Chicago. He says many people go every day to the US through the fence right here. That's why it's open. It's a longer way to go, take us a few hours of slow driving. But there's nobody over there, only a few rangers from the park. They'd just think we're campers, because illegals crossing here never go in trailers like this."

"Probably for a reason."

* * *

The Refuge Ranger lies in the cool of the soft-sand wash, listening to the crackling rustle of the thorny ocotillo overhead and the bat wings shushing through the night air. Then the belching chug of an old Suburban, laboring through the drifting sand, heavy with a half-ton load. People or pot? It passes, seen but not seeing, blinder than the long-nosed bats shirring overhead, the sweet smell of new rope giving away its cargo. Next, a rhythmic rasping of cloth—jeans—punctuated by the soft thud of sneakers, nearing along the smugglers' road. She counts them by footfall—six, seven, eight—and then checks her accuracy as they pass with brisk strides, still only one night out. They don't see her. They never do.

Hours later she is awakened by another sound, farther away: the soft whine of wheels spinning hopelessly in the sand. Cursing softly, she pulls herself from the sleeping bag and makes her still stiff way out of the wash and up the stony rise, from which, lying flat, she can see back south over half a mile or so of the road to where a massive red truck is caught in a drift of moon dust sand. Sand it might have handled but for its huge fifth-wheel trailer, sunk into that powder like an anchor so that the whole rig looks as if it is being dragged down under the surreally still, moon-lit waves. An older man and woman climb slowly down from the truck and stand together, staring for far longer than it should take to reach the obvious conclusion. Nothing can be done without first unhitching the trailer, and even then, it will not be easy to get the truck back on its feet.

The man, tall and gray with a paunch, moves reluctantly to the trailer door, opening it slowly and then moving to the side. A small boy leaps out onto the sand, followed by one man or woman after another, each stepping gingerly, reluctantly into the engulfing drift. The ranger nearly whistles in amazement, counting them as they emerge.

"That's a new one. Snowbird *coyotes*!"

* * *

Ruby, carried along thus far on her newfound will, now stares dumbly at the rig. But Ned has awakened from the dream, faced with just the sort of problem he can handle.

"We can get out of this. And if your waiter is right, the crossroad should be just up ahead. And from there it's about twenty-five miles across into Organ Pipe Park and on to Route Eighty-five. And about a half-hour's drive to Ajo."

Ned says all this calmly, comforted by the clarity and mechanical nature of the situation, With the wiry little boy jumping at his side like a happy monkey, he lowers the jacks and settles the footpads as firmly as possible in the sand, and then sends the boy into the back of the truck to detach the hitch. The two of them crank, slowly hoisting the front end of the trailer—unwilling in the slipping sand—until it stands bow-legged, swaying above the truck bed.

The passengers need no instructions; the men squeeze together and shoulder up to the back end of the truck, as Ned climbs into the cab and starts the engine. On the second heave, the truck is out, flat on its feet, the motor humming competently, awaiting its next task.

Ruby is still just looking defeated, unable to see the next step.

"We do it in two loads," Ned explains. "First trip without the trailer. I can carry them out to the good road, hide them there some place and then come back for the trailer and the second load. Keep them in the back of the truck so the trailer stays light. We put the strongest men in that group, in case we need to shift the trailer."

"What if we run into anyone on the way? By the second trip it'll be daylight."

"The first trip is riskier, no place to hide anyone, but it will be dark. On the second trip, if we see anyone, we can put them all back in the trailer. We're just lost snowbirds. Camped in the park and making for Ajo."

The Ranger, too curious to return to her sleeping bag, watches the flurry of activity, no longer surprised by what she sees. Whether for reasons of greed or humanity, the old couple are clearly not considering abandoning the others, who space themselves about the rear of the trailer and carefully rock, lift and then swivel it to the side, letting the wheels down on harder ground.

Ned points his flashlight down at his Arizona map, looking up again at the surrounding wilderness, an infinite expanse of moonlit gray desert divided only by a series of parallel white granite mountain walls dozens of miles apart, gleaming even in the dark, each of them slicing northeast to southwest. He turns to the little boy, who hasn't left his side, and asks his name.

"I'm Lalo."

"The road we took up here certainly isn't on this—or probably any—map, but if you take a look at those mountain ranges there, you can see clear enough about where we are."

Lalo stares in blinking incomprehension. The only map he has known is that of Mexico, an abstraction like the flag, signifying by shape as the other did by colors. But then, looking more closely, he realizes that the two rows of peaked lines to which Ned is pointing are a drawing, not unlike one he might do himself, of the glistening granite walls in the distance. Then, it's as if the ground has dropped out from under him as he rockets skyward, dizzy with understanding. The world around him shrinks back and flattens, and the map undulates into life, rising into mountains, sinking into gullies and washes. Still following Ned's calloused finger as it scratches along the paper to the right, he sees himself and the old man moving through that dimensioned world, along that dotted line.

"What do you think, Lalo?"

But the boy is already out the door, hurrying to the back of the truck to explain to the others that they are doing fine, that they are right there on the map and that the map will take them out to the highway. He rejoins Ned in the cab, alight with excitement.

"*Ya*! Let's go!"

Ned chuckles and, and with half their passengers crammed in the back of the truck, rumbles off into the dying night, trying to make time while the darkness holds. Lalo watches intently out the window as they climb and descend over fields of wind-rounded stones, past forests of stately saguaro cactus standing like black sentries in the night, and fields of waving, thin-limbed ocotillo. "When I make a map," Lalo thinks, "it will have all this."

They roll carefully across the lava flows, sheets of smooth or bubbly black rock, the tires spitting out jagged fragments that ring hollow against the demonic landscape. Then comes more sand. The road surrenders to ever wider and deeper stretches of softly alluring, powdery "moon dust." Though no desert driver, Ned has pushed his truck through everything Alberta has to offer and knows enough to keep at least one wheel on solider ground, even if that means a slantwise run through the greasewood or mesquite that is hedging the road. The passengers in the back hold on as best they can, and only twice get out and meet the truck a hundred yards or so farther on. Lalo never dismounts and is thrilled by every gut-jolting passage.

Ruby sits with the one woman who had remained behind, trying to communicate. She realizes with some pride that, despite herself, she has picked up quite a few Spanish words at the church, at the tortilla shop, and in the streets and supermarket aisles of Yuma. Sentences are out of the question, but a noun or two coupled with an acted-out verb is enough to frame a simple question or reply. The other woman hasn't a word of English. Spanish is in fact her second language, learned from the age of five in a classroom she left by the time she was nine. This she has not succeeded in communicating to Ruby. But Ruby does recognize one word.

"*Zapotec.*"

The woman points smiling to herself and utters a greeting in her native tongue.

"Zapotec," Ruby repeats. "I know that word. It's a rug!"

She has seen them in the Algodones tourist shops and tries to draw one in the sand.

The woman nods happily and, grabbing two saguaro ribs from the ground nearby, thrusts them in the sand and sits before them, passing a stone shuttle in and out through the imaginary yarn. They both laugh at the clarity of the pantomime and Ruby looks around at the other migrants, suddenly aware that each has a story if you only knew the word with which it begins.

* * *

"Better get them all in the trailer. Border Patrol coming up the road."

Ruby is startled by the sound of English, but when she looks up to see a young woman in uniform, her heart seizes up and falls like a stone into her quaking belly. The others freeze where they sit, mostly leaning up against the side of the trailer, smoking cigarettes and watching the night sky. Somehow this woman has managed to move up on them like a ghost. The uniform must mean the end of their passage.

But Ruby, rising quickly if shakily to her feet, replays the woman's words, and animal fear gives way to confusion. She looks past the uniform and sees a long-limbed, boyishly slender, young woman, with close-set eyes sparkling in the dark. She is smiling.

"I'm a Park Ranger. Like I said, the Border Patrol is just down the road there, so get everyone inside the trailer and you go in with them. I'll handle things out here."

Ruby hesitates, but then, eased by the Ranger's calm and steady tone, rounds up her charges with as much authority as she can muster and sends them all back into the trailer. Before she closes the door behind them, the Ranger leans in and says,

"*Soy una amiga. Ya llega la Migra, que quédense por dentro, silencioso. ¿Me entienden?*" Ruby knew "amiga" and "Migra." She could guess the rest.

"Hey Tobias, Reinhart." The Ranger greets the agents as they pull up to the trailer.

"Do you believe it? Fucking snowbirds! I picked up the trail south of here."

"Yeah, us too." Reinhart nods a thick head topped with a salt-and-pepper crew cut. "Couldn't believe the sign, you know, all those wheels dragging ass through the sand? Thought we were on to the world's record dope run!"

Reinhardt leans heavily against the patrol car, but Tobias, eyes still curious, strolls toward the trailer door.

The Ranger watches out of the corner of her eye and continues.

"So, then I came over the hill there, and what do I find? Abandoned goddamn fifth wheel. Somehow, they got the truck out from under it and turned back south. Probably had no idea where they were."

She gestures toward the set of truck tracks she had herself just enough time to make with her own vehicle, looping back into Ed's northward leading track before leaving it parked in plain sight fifty yards ahead of them.

"I'm working the Refuge north of here all night, counting bats, so I'll let you know if I see anything strange in that direction."

Reinhart yawns and opens the patrol car door, just as his partner reaches for the one on the trailer.

"Come on, Tobias, let's go south again. We must have missed their tracks turning off on one of those other smuggler roads."

Just then their satellite phone rings. Reinhart answers.

"Yeah, yeah, got it. We'll be there in time for our shift."

Rinehart hangs up and looks over at Tobias, whose narrow frame bends over the trailer, a long-fingered hand dropping onto the handle. The ranger holds her breath.

"Fuck it," Rinehart groans. "We're not going south after all. The new boss is rotating everyone around. Everybody's doing turns at the checkpoint and our shift begins in two hours. So, we've got just about enough time to drag our asses out of the sand here."

Tobias turns back from the trailer and moves toward the patrol car. "Fucking guy thinks we're having too good a time out here."

They laugh in self-recognition.

"Do you believe that woman?" Tobias remarks, looking out the window toward the ranger as they pull away.

"If that's what she is. One of a kind! We're chasing fucking illegals and dope all night, and she's counting goddamn bats!" Reinhart laughs, gunning the engine and leaving a swath of broken greasewood in their wake.

* * *

"Do you think we should give your Ranger friend a cut? After all, she saved our bacon, that's for sure, eh?"

Ned and Ruby are, unbelievably, on the road. A real road, among a steady stream of motor homes, trailers, and fifth wheels heading back to Phoenix from a weekend on the Sonoran beach. Ned's second run went smoothly enough, save for the great stretch of moon dust. But many hands shortened the work; Ned and little Lalo turned the men into a road crew, covering the sand trap with a kind of boardwalk of ocotillo limbs, saguaro ribs, and mesquite branches. After that, the dirt and gravel road that looped through Organ Pipe felt like a superhighway. Then it was out the exit with the overnighters from the park, and on to route 85. Ajo is only thirty easy miles ahead, and they will meet Lobo on a road just outside Gila Bend, another half hour beyond that.

"No, I'm sure she doesn't expect any money. I swear she did it for the hell of it. Maybe we'll see her again, though, if we stay in Ajo, at the Shady 'K'. What do you say we hole up there? Like they say in the movies." Ruby's words were a giddy avalanche, bravado belied by a knife-in-the-gut tension that was finally beginning to soften. Ned was smiling over at his "Bonnie," trying to look the Clyde part himself, though his sweaty fist was threatening to slide off the steering wheel.

"Uh-huh."

"And Verna told me there's a woman there who gives classes on scrapbooking. You know, where you learn how to put all the family photos and cards and such into a book."

"You need lessons for that?"

They both laugh, and Ruby looks down at Lalo, who raises his head groggily from her lap, then up at Ned, who whispers,

"I didn't tell you, he's alone. And he wasn't in Lobo's group at all. He's a street kid from somewhere near the border and was hanging out at the Café. That's why he's got some English. I guess the others probably thought he was working for us!"

"You mean he's a stowaway?"

"And with no particular place to go."

The boy was now fully awake and beaming out the window, still making maps.

"Lalo," Ruby said to the child, "is that short for something?"

"*Sí, Eduardo*. Like him."

"Junior!" She laughs. And then stops herself.

"Up ahead! It's a Border Patrol checkpoint."

Lalo scoots over behind the seats, pulling a length of canvas tarp over himself.

"Don't worry," said Ned, gulping as if he has just taken a good jolt of whiskey to steady his nerves. "They're just waving everyone through. Everyone who looks like us."

True. Occasionally, an agent smiles in an RV window, but everyone is sailing on.

Inside the checkpoint cabin, agent Rinehart sips coffee as the first gray light brings the shadowy desert into soft focus. Hard to enjoy the moment though, under the watchful eye of the new boss. He has been sent to put an end to their days of freewheeling through the desert—"you're doing far more damage to the flora and fauna than to the smuggling." But they are facing more than such blunt observations and new procedures. Orozco, a local, knows the scene better than anyone, and he's a bear of a man who backs up any order with an intimidating, looming presence.

"Well, Chief, as you can see, it's quiet enough now, just the last strays coming back from Rocky Point." Rinehart observes, with his best attempt at an ingratiating smile, nodding toward the red truck and fifth wheel that has just pulled up. Orozco follows his gaze, watching the rig intently as it slows over the speed bumps and comes to a careful halt. Tobias, who was on line duty, steps up and leans wearily into the vehicle while another agent walks briskly about the rig with the dope-sniffing Alsatian.

"How're ya folks? Down at Rocky Point?"

"That's right," the driver responds, grinning easily.

"Lovely time," said the woman next to him, with a warm grandmotherly smile.

Tobias looks back to see the sniffer dog lope around the rig. No drugs. And yet there is something about the trailer, something that makes him walk over for a closer look. He stands staring at the door and is about to reach for the handle when he feels Orozco coming up behind him. Stifling a yawn, he walks back to the truck window.

"Right, you folks have a great day!"

The old man nods, breathes out, and puts the truck in gear.

"Hold on a minute, sir." Orozco is now alongside and leaning into the passenger side window. A knowing smile spreads slowly across his wide face, for he has noted the loud scrape as the trailer passed over the speed bump, sending back a pretty little shower of sparks.

"Riding awfully low, aren't you? Mind if we take a look inside?"

5

Endangered Species

Fig. 5.1 Photograph by Maeve Hickey

Clyde Kastenbader pulls his brim forward, eclipsing an albino chipmunk face God never intended for the desert, hikes up his silver-studded belt, and, with the longest strides his stumpy limbs can manage, makes his habitual way across the town green to *el Rincon*. Even with high-heeled boots and an eagle-feathered, tall crown Texas Stetson, Clyde still falls well short of average height. But his every gesture is meant to insist that if smaller than most, he is larger than life: a view shared by the coterie of local idlers gathered around the bar like gnats on a cow pad, waiting to enjoy his largesse.

But Clyde's expansive mood is deflated by a fretting call from Evi.

"She's some kind of freaky ghost out there, *hombre*. Sleeps in the washes. Sees and hears everything. Frightened the fuck out of some *pollos* coming through Temporal Pass. *¡Les dio agua!* They swear they saw an old Indian lady with her, hanging back in the dark. Now there're stories all over Sonora about female spirits floating through the desert at night. Whatever about *migrantes*, she ain't gonna be so accommodating if she comes across one of our loads!"

They meet that evening at La Margarita's across the border in Sonoyta, where, over platters of *gorditas* piled with *barbacoa*, Clyde lays out his plan. The key is an unassuming ungulate, darling of the eco-nuts and bane of the ranchers and wilderness joyriders, that little "ghost of the desert," the Sonoran pronghorn.

Evi is incredulous.

"*Un chingado ciervo*! Fucking deer? How's that gonna work?"

But Clyde is glowing bright pink with confidence, his tiny yellowy blue eyes dancing in anticipated revenge.

"*Welcome to Ajo.*"

Lucy slowed before the pebble-pocked sign heralding the end of her cross-country pilgrimage from an awkward, friendless childhood in the cramped, civilized East to the promise of adult freedom in the open, wilderness West. She cocked a long, thin face sideways, like a roadrunner considering a snake. There was something vaguely sinister about the dancing saguaro adorning the sign, its weathered smile more like a leer. But she continued, following the road between twin colossi of mine waste studded with bits of rusted machinery, haunting the entrance of the town like grisly wonders of the ancient world. As if some Ozymandias of the western desert had mistaken his brief rock- and soul-crushing reign for immortality.

In town, the tarmac shimmered in the unforgiving noon light, taking her past a dusty RV court, stores long closed or obstinately open, and tiny frame houses with parched lawns enlivened by ceramic gnomes and purple whirligigs. At the far end of this sorry line-up, as if dropped from the sky, the Refuge Headquarters presented its hygienically impersonal brick and glass front to passers-by and its back to the wild desert that waited patiently to engulf it, and the rest of the town, in its own good time.

A blast of conditioned air chilled the gritty sweat on Lucy's back, making her feel as dirty as the elderly lady volunteer greeter clearly thought she was. Beyond the counter, scientists and clerical staff were busy in their own world, reading computer screens through thick glasses and rising to fix themselves cups of coffee. She was trying to imagine herself among them when the manager, a gaunt, pleasantly lazy Coloradan, came out to greet her.

He was new himself, as he explained, having taken the post for a better deal on an impending retirement only to find himself uneasily presiding over close to a million barely accessible acres with fifty-six miles of Mexican border: an immense but fragile wilderness trampled by smugglers, migrants, and the Border Patrol. In this chaos, his job was to ensure the survival of several officially endangered species, most notably the little Sonoran pronghorn.

"There're only a couple dozen still out there."

He looked defeated, though unable to resist an ironic smile.

"Pretty much everybody hates us. Wildlife groups want us to do more for the critters. Townsfolk think we do far too much: kicking out their cattle and banning their quads. Then there's all those miles of border with illegals crossing all the time. The liberals say 'give 'em water and sandwiches' and conservatives say 'shoot 'em, build a Berlin wall, or dig a moat and fill it with rattlesnakes.'"

As "field ranger," Lucy found she could avoid both the office and the stark comforts and retiree neighbors of her tin home in Shady K trailer court. The desert turned out to be as much a refuge for her as it was for the other wildlife, and as autumn tempered the heat, her day hikes grew to three-day treks. She found her own desert peace and pace:

long-legging up the saguaro-studded flanks of the ranges that divided the desert into a series of harsh, waterless basins the maps called valleys. Less lonely than in her trailer, she slept comfortably in the cool sands of the washes: stream beds that saw water only when the brief but battering summer rains scoured broad highways and steep dirt canyons into the desert surface. In this so-called wilderness, Lucy was surprised to discover not only groups of migrants (to whom she gave water and directions) but also the many traces of former human life: from old mine shafts and the remnants of corrals and wells to far older and more mysterious drawings etched into boulders and, in the most desolate stretches of creosote flatland, several acres of pottery shards swirled and lined in black and ochre. Though beyond her remit, she couldn't help wondering about the people whose home she was sharing, whose spectral presence she might feel in an evening breeze or in the serene eye of a coyote.

* * *

Clyde Kastenbader had a lucky start in Ajo when, years before, he rolled across the border from his exile in Sonora with an ambitious wife, a prematurely voluptuous daughter and, most important, a functioning tow-truck. When cars broke down in the desert it was a long and expensive way out and it wasn't long before the little family had worked their way into a trim doublewide, parked on a rented, two-acre parcel on the edge of town with plenty of space for "Big K Towing's" capacious metal shed.

Just in time to witness the town's demise.

It was a mortal match of few moves. The price of copper dropped like mercury in a Montana winter. The Company cut salaries. The workers fought back with a long and costly strike. The Company closed the mine, fired everyone and put their rented, shit-box houses on the block for a few thousand dollars apiece. Game over. Apart from a handful of merchants and struggling family ranches, copper had been the only show in town, and it looked like Ajo was destined to join the gallery of Arizona ghost towns: another set of pits, slag heaps, and rusting ore cars left behind in the periodic glacial retreat of mining.

But Clyde's bride, squat and practical Divina Luz, saw other possibilities. Every fall there was a steady flow of recreational vehicles on their way from Phoenix to the Mexican beaches on the Sea of Cortez, as well as those folks escaping the frigid winters of Minnesota and Manitoba looking for an inexpensive place to hang a straw hat till the spring thaw. Why not Ajo? They could buy a few miners' homes for eventual resale, meanwhile renting them out as winter residences. And there was that five-acre parcel on the edge of town that would be perfect for an RV park. If only they had the funds.

Money was out there in the vast unpeopled, lightly patrolled desert—a drug-runner's paradise. But that cash fell and flowed like the summer rains, nurturing only those well-placed in its path. Now and again, a trickle reached Clyde when the sheriff sent him to retrieve cars abandoned by runners in the dunes. Just towing fees, until one such mission on the Reservation when Clyde, having hooked up an old Suburban, spied a neatly tied package on the floor under the passenger seat and, whistling softly through his twisted teeth, tossed the brick of weed into his truck.

The next morning, the reticent, young Deputy Sheriff banged into Big K Towing and, after a desultory rummage through a bin of remaindered tools, leaned over the counter,

"Wondering if you might have a package for me?"

Without a word, Kastenbader retrieved and dropped the unopened parcel on the counter between them. The Deputy nodded, sliding it into a large paper bag and leaving an envelope on the counter, turned and shuffled out the door.

It became a near weekly event, with far more weed and cash per adventure, till Clyde had the down payment for the first phase of Kastenbader Enterprises. Shady KRV Park was soon a favorite spot for wintering "full-timers" and younger families seeking a few days' respite on the way south to Mexico. And the half dozen little houses they bought proved popular rentals for those retirees who liked their homes without wheels. While most of the locals watched in dazed wonder from their collapsing front porches, rising only to collect their food stamps and disability checks, the Kastenbaders opened and expanded their stores, catering to the new community of visitors. But the locals were not forgotten. They were welcome to haul their dirty clothing into the Shady K's coin-operated laundry room. And there was Big K Liquors, where Divina Luz accepted food stamps for beer and tequila, giving three dollars' value for four dollars' worth, duly transferred to the Circle K till. Buying that franchise had been another of her ideas. After all, it already bore what might as well serve as the family crest.

Clyde had learned in Mexico that mockery and admiration were not mutually exclusive and had since developed his costume and behavior to a trademark extreme. In vivid contrast to the increasingly dour Divina Luz, he burst into any room like a vaudeville act, barking out greetings loud enough to penetrate the background blare of *Radio Ranchera*. However, if Clyde wore his arrogance with the same natural ease as the eagle feather gracing his oversized hat, his performance was in fact fragile. His belief in himself needed constant affirmation—with anything from shameless toadying to spiteful envy. He expected attention, and he usually got it. But he was plagued by a self-doubt as persistent and irritating as a hot rash on the back of his neck and nobody could set that rash to itching like Jake Evers.

Ajo was home to a handful of old ranchers still chasing a few cattle through what little land was left to them, a melancholy aristocracy clinging to a sense of themselves they had learned as much in the cinema as in the saddle. Jake Evers was the most authentic of these, a good-natured older man, cowboy handsome but with a disappointed, self-deprecating smile and the ironic air of a distinguished actor crossing the stage long after the engagement has been canceled. He would preside when the ranchers were gathered around the bar at the *Elks* to reminisce and regret, and Kastenbader, who would hang back in the shadows, would never hear any reference to *his Ajo*. It was a disregard that fueled Clyde's determination to see his daughter Lupe married to Evers' son, an otherwise unpromising, pimply adolescent with none of his father's earthy grace or rustic charm. That ambition made no sense to Divina Luz, who saw Evers as simply washed up and would have much preferred to marry her daughter into a family of Phoenix Mexicans with a wholesale distribution business.

Clyde had hoped to secure Lupe's future, as well as enter the town's fiesta hall of fame, with a blowout *quinceañera*, a Mexican fifteenth birthday party to rival any wedding. He erected a cavernous marquee beside his towing shed, festooned with great bunches of the spring bougainvillea then blooming purple, red, and yellow throughout the town. There would be live music, mountains of food—consisting mainly of anything that could be wrapped in a flour tortilla and fried deep and long—and a heroic flow of beer. A full-page announcement in the *Copper Chronicle* threw the party open to all and sundry, but a hand-delivered note invited the Evers family to join the Kastenbaders at the table of honor.

They never showed. Clyde spent the night watching Lupe pressing ample breasts into the willing adolescent bodies of trailer trash, *cholos*, and Indians, some of whom had picked up the Mexican art of achieving total body contact in even the fastest of dances, wearing Lupe like an article of clothing as, legs interlocked, they whirled about the floor to the brassy Sinaloan polkas.

In the eyes of Ajo folks, the *quinceañera* had been a memorable success, but Clyde was still nursing his resentment over Evers when, a few weeks later he suddenly lost the income, and prestige, that came with the drug-laden vehicles he had been hauling out of the Reservation. The Deputy Sheriff disappeared, and it was weeks before his desiccated body was found out on the Reservation. Divina Luz was by then ably managing the Kastenbader retail holdings, but they had both grown used to the ready cash their other business had regularly supplied. So, there followed one lean and painful year; Divina Luz bore down on her indebted customers while Clyde avoided his Mexican drinking buddies, fearing they no longer saw him as fit to figure in a *narcotraficante corrido*.

Then Divina Luz's brother Kiki put Clyde in touch with Evi Gomez Portillo, a wolf-eyed player from Sinaloa, who had already established a new drug route to the west of Ajo, through the Refuge.

"That's where you come in," Evi explained to Clyde. "Most of the time there is nobody out there and the boys can drive the loads right up to the Interstate and on to Phoenix. But if the way is blocked, I would like another possibility. You find them a place to drop their load, and then you pick it up and hide it in town where my boys can get it later."

Clyde dropped a pudgy finger on the map Evi had spread out between them. "Here's where they'll go, through Temporal Pass and down into this country. Close enough to town to make easy runs and plenty of places to stash your loads among the old ranch and Indian village ruins." He indicated a deeply ravined *bajada* just over the border in the Refuge.

"Rangers?"

"No problem. There's nothing much goin' in that corner. No pronghorn. There's a crazy old Indian lady lives a few miles off, but she sure as fuck won't be hikin' over the pass and down into those ravines. And the land over on the other side is the Bureau of Land Management (BLM), federal land where Jake Evers's got his lease. He's runnin' cattle in there, so the hunters and tourists are fenced out." *If damned Evers were a different sort of man, he'd be perfectly placed for the run: in with feed and out with dope.* Clyde hadn't forgiven the rancher for the snub, but he still dreamed of uniting their families.

With wads of cash back in his pocket, Clyde was once again Clown Emperor of Ajo: a benevolent, extravagant, hard-ass fucker, who'd curse you up and down but buy you a drink. The stuff of legend, who had realized his potential in the United Fucking States of America. His new business hummed along without a hitch through the next few years; Evi's men would drop a load behind an abandoned well, Clyde would retrieve and haul it out to his storage shed on the edge of town, where he'd stack the marijuana among bales of hay. All good.

Until it wasn't.

* * *

It had been a profitable winter season for the tourist trade and Clyde paused on the green to consider putting up a bandstand before striding purposefully toward the Ajo Rose. Just inside, with a dusty hat pushed back on his head, Jake Evers was checking the paper for beef prices while toying with half-cooked hunks of dough trailing globs of kryptonite-green Jell-O. Lucky for him, he wasn't paying much attention to his food. Unlike the clutch of white-haired women surrounding the next table, noisily delighted with their heaping portions of something the menu described as Italian. Their flat, friendly Minnesota voices boomed a chorus of hellos to the landlord of Shady KRV Park as Kastenbader passed their table. He smiled and hung back, waiting for Evers to look up and note his passing. He didn't.

At the back of the room, Evi sat waiting in a corner booth. He had removed wrap-around sunglasses from an ashy face creased with consternation to better examine the contents of the bowl set before him, teasing a few scraps of wilting lettuce. He looked up to scowl at Kastenbader, who slid into the bench opposite.

"*Tenemos problemas, amigo.* It's that *muchacha* from the Refuge who is wandering around in the desert. Doesn't she know it's dangerous out there? That fucking ranger is going to mess things up for us. She is living in your goddamn trailer court, no?"

* * *

"*Today O'odham Festival.*"

A better option than another conspicuously solo lunch in town, wrestling with a wizened chicken-fried steak, feeling the Shady K ladies' eyes weighing up her scant form. Not endurable. Besides, Lucy couldn't help feeling some tickly flurry of excitement at the word "festival." She hung a hard right off the tarmac and bounced over the pebbly sand up to a dozen trucks and SUVs scattered about a cluster of tents and ramadas, joining the modest mob of locals who had taken a break from porch-sitting to gorge on Native American heritage, in the shape of fry bread.

A wad of crisped dough glistening with honey and grease in hand, Lucy entered a tent over whose entrance a sign promised "*Culture.*" A couple of middle-aged white women in long denim skirts were milling around a folding table with rows of wooden bowls, each with bits of seed, bark, or leaves, and an unpronounceable O'odham name card. The two elderly Indian women presiding showed no inclination to address them, but one turned to Lucy.

"Go ahead, honey, you can pick one up."

Lucy's thin lips pulled tight into a concentrated grimace as she plucked one of the tiny blackish seeds from the wooden dish and, bringing her hand up to within inches of her unblinking eye, rolled it about between her fingers until she had a distinct mental picture of its papery form.

"You know what that is?"

The old lady's black eyes sparkled in a pinched and deeply lined light sienna face, incongruously framed by a frilly collared polka dot dress below, and a tight maroon and gray permanent above. As if she had pushed her head through a cut-out form for a comic photo.

"*Carnegiea gigante*. Saguaro seeds. Kangaroo rat food this time of year."

"Not if we got 'em first!"

The old lady grinned like a mischievous schoolgirl, "Make a kind of paste from them, tastes real good. You're the new one at the Refuge who wears a uniform like the men! I see you walking up from Shady K. I am Viola. Viola Duckworth. Welcome to Ajo."

"Lucy Villary," she said, extending her hand.

Viola's grip was surprisingly strong. She spoke without drawing breath: her voice low, her accent a slow lilt over the local Indian speech, as if she had been sent away to a Southern boarding school for a brief but important time. Her words were so carefully and proudly enunciated that grammatical errors seemed legitimate and distinctive speech forms.

"We call that seed *Bahidaj Kaij*. My mother used to say white folks think up funny names for things so other people won't be able to keep them in their heads. But I suppose we just want to know whether you can eat the thing or not!"

She laughed out loud and rising to shuffle her display into a large black, patent leather purse, announced, "We are about done here, honey. Let's you take me back home to where I can tell you about the seeds and such and you can tell me your names for them." She hooked her arm through Lucy's and headed for the Trooper.

Driving south, Viola directed a silent Lucy off the tarmac for a washboard dirt road and then on over more challenging terrain, weaving between clumps of creosote, through fence gaps and across washes, her head lolling happily out the window as if engaged in casual communion with the landscape, until they emerged into a clearing within a mesquite bosque where a '70s' vintage trailer was parked on a level stretch of stony ground alongside an Oldsmobile of the same era. Though still in possession of all its wheels, the sad, listing hulk had about it the deep inertia the desert heat seemed to engender in machines and living creatures.

"My late husband's car. Very comfortable ride."

Lucy followed Viola into the kitchen and found a seat on one of three plaid plastic-on-chrome chairs. Her host dropped into another and rooted out the little plastic bags of herbaceous matter, arranging them in a row on the chipped Formica table. Feeling that she was in class again, Lucy reached for the little notebook she kept in her back pocket and wrote as Viola spoke, marking down first the Latin, then the O'odham name, followed by a few words that she hoped would later recall Viola's meandering narratives, which included recipes, sharp comments about relatives, and ironic asides.

"You see, honey…"

Viola summed up, leaning back in her chair and gesturing grandly out the open window.

"The people are not on their land, so they have forgotten everything."

She swept a long and bony arm to the south, where several hundred square miles lay under the jurisdiction of various branches of the federal government.

"We always lived here, and moved from one camp to another, for the season, but also over the years. There were never many of us *Hia-Ced* people, and so we just about made it, hunting, raising a few crops by flooding a field. And gathering these."

She pointed a gnarled finger at the bags of plant bits.

"And here was our last place."

Viola climbed out of her seat and, Lucy following, banged out the door and pointing around her to the bails of rusted wire, collapsed sections of dry mud and ocotillo walls, pieces of machinery and lengths of indecipherable metal and wood scattered among the contorted mesquite trees, named the people evoked by these bits of debris, nodding with resignation at the meager traces of their lives.

"We all lived here till you folks moved us off…"

Lucy realized that they were in fact a mile or two inside the Refuge boundary, where even a visit required a permit. But it looked as though Viola had been, and would be, there for a long while. Probably, the manager felt it wasn't worth the trouble to try to move her.

"They told us that we had to leave, on account of the pronghorn. That's something maybe you can explain to me. When we were here, there was plenty of those critters. They weren't as easy to hunt as the deer. Wouldn't go into any place they couldn't see all around themselves."

Viola, cutting a strange figure in the polka dot dress, spun slowly on a sneakered foot, mimicking the searching vigilance of the pronghorn.

"We killed some alright. But like I said, there was always plenty of them around. Till you people started protecting them. Now there's hardly any of them left. That's puzzling!"

She turned a wide-eyed, innocent face to Lucy, belied by a slight tremor in her lips.

Viola mounted the steps into the trailer, talking over her shoulder as she went.

"I'm making some coffee, honey."

She slipped a delicate, cracked cup and saucer in front of Lucy, settled back down with her own, and poured bubbling water into an unpromising heap of odorless black powder nestled inside each cup. Lucy tried not to squirm under Viola's searching stare, and when the old lady reached suddenly across the table, she feared for a moment that she would be struck for whatever unwitting part she had in the loss of *Hia-Ced* land. But Viola caught up a curling strand of Lucy's honey-colored hair and pulled it up and away from her face.

"Why don't you fix yourself up? You have a soft, pretty face. Lovely. It's terrible to make a lady wear a uniform like that."

It was the first time anyone had used the word "pretty" to describe her and Lucy wondered if it could be in any way true. As for the ranger uniform, that had been a definite plus. No inevitably bad choices of clothing; no appraising and disparaging looks from other women. Her hair she kept neat and clean, fearing that any more effort would yield diminishing returns. But she had never put anything like makeup on her face. Once, her mother had dared to suggest she try some: "It'll make your eyes bigger and your nose a little less long." But Viola seemed to be suggesting an enhancement rather than a disguise. Lucy couldn't help smiling.

"That's it, honey, you've got sparkly eyes. Real pretty. Now, you go ahead and tell them you can't wear the damn uniform all the time. And you come here tomorrow morning, so we can go out and I can show you where all those seeds come from."

They were interrupted by a series of creaks, shuffles, and bangs; Lucy twisted around in time to see a man emerge from the shadowy depths of the trailer. He was lanky like Viola, but much whiter, though with black, Indian eyes. His rumpled and dirty sleeveless T-shirt completed the distinctive look of a near forty-year-old thoroughly accustomed to and reasonably content with reduced circumstances. He didn't cut a striking figure.

"This is my nephew Francisco, honey. We call him Chico. He's takin' a break from … whatever he's takin' a break from. This here is Lucy, who has come here to learn about the plants."

Chico slid sleepily into the remaining dining chair and opened one eye, then the other, then suddenly broke into a broad, surprisingly charming grin. He reached over and touched Lucy's hand.

"Welcome."

Viola shot him a "what are you up to?" look, and then turned to address Lucy, who felt a liquid warmth spread up her arm as Chico slowly lifted his hand.

"Time you got back, honey, before it gets too dark."

* * *

However early she arrived at Viola's trailer, Lucy found the old lady ready—sack cotton dress, hi-top sneakers, floppy straw hat, an old shoulder bag holding a bottle of water, knives, and a small pair of scissors—and anxious to set off into the terrain of her childhood, following the ghost of her mother's mother. Lucy wondered whether Viola had come to resemble her and asked what the old woman had been like.

"Small, round, and dark as a berry, just like my mom," Viola said.

Lucy looked surprised.

"No, she was nothing like me, honey. I get my height from my father's side; he was Josiah Duckworth. His mother was an Evers." That's right—Viola read Lucy's expression—Jake Evers is a cousin of mine. Our grandparents were brother and sister.

Lucy had taken Evers for the epitome of the white rancher.

"Honey, we are more mixed up here than we let on. Jake's own mother was a Mexican woman from down *Caborca*. It's not that those people were so open-minded; it's just that there wasn't enough white women to go round. Most all the old Anglo ranching families have a Mexican woman or two mixed in. My dad though was the only one of them to take up with an Indian woman, or at least to halfway claim his children."

When they first set out together, Lucy didn't imagine that the old lady was still capable of even one day in the desert. But Viola's long and easy stride never slackened. Day after day they tramped through fields of red-flowered ocotillos, across the crusted or yielding sands, picking and naming sprigs and pods as they went. When they had combed what seemed like every inch of Viola's childhood landscape, they ventured further, visiting the subtler traces of *Hia-Ced O'odham* far longer gone. They walked the washes, sandy paths between verges thick with ironwood, mesquite, grasses, and brittle bush. Sometimes, when Viola was silent Lucy would sink into her habitual desert trance, at once removed and yet aware of the merest rustle of a small lizard in the brush. Then Viola might suddenly burst into laughing, reminiscing talk as she bent down to pluck a leaf or stretched up to pull a pod, sometimes crushing it for Lucy to smell, or poking it raw into her startled mouth. Sharp, musky, lemony, even sweet, though she had seen and heard much, Lucy was learning the tastes of the desert.

One day, they embarked on a long hike, arriving at Christmas Pass just in time to pitch camp under the stars. Lucy unrolled a thin sleeping bag on the sandy wash alongside the tattered sheet and army blanket Viola had brought in a roll slung across her back. Once a fire of dried mesquite branches was crackling against the violet sky, Viola skewered some hot dogs on green sticks, jamming the ends into the sand so that the meat sputtered over the fire.

"Lucy, honey," Viola said, as she carefully laid out slices of bread across her sheet, "in all our walks out here we surely did see a lot of plants and creatures, eh? Even those bighorns walking up and over the ridge by Charlie Bell Mountain. The tail of a lion disappearin' into the canyon—if that's what it was. And whenever we slept out here, we did see all manner of human beings passin' in the night. Most of them just poor folks on their way north to bad jobs. But did we see a single pronghorn?"

Lucy agreed that they had not.

"Well, that's 'cause they are not here. Why? 'Cause they are all up in their favorite place. Do you know where that is?"

Lucy had a good idea, knowing that in those dry days the pronghorns would browse for fresh shoots in the one place where the desert's dry crust was regularly broken.

"Up in the bombing range?"

"That's right, honey. Smack in the fiery wake of their baddest bombs."

At that moment two fighter jets chased each other in smoking arcs, thundering their way across the sky right over their heads. It was a common occurrence, since most fighter pilots battling through the skies in the Middle East were trained right there in the Goldwater Bombing Range, just north of the Refuge.

"You know, honey, you got to laugh. Every year you close down everything. Nobody can drive or even walk through these lands from March to July. Pronghorn fawning, they say. Easy to disturb them." Her eyes follow the jet trails looping over the low peaks of the Pintas. "Can you show me any soldier that has seen and heard more planes, more bombs, and more missiles than your pronghorn?"

* * *

Walking with Viola or alone, Lucy would lose herself in the desert. But her normally empty sleep was disturbed by inarticulate sounds and visions that drifted about the edge of her mind. She couldn't quite admit they had something to do with Viola's nephew, Chico, of whom Lucy has only caught suggestive glimpses since their first meeting—so curtailed by Viola. She saw him in town on her way home one evening, coming out of *El Rincon*, followed, she thought, by that young, blondish Mexican girl bursting out of her blouse. And several times, when she and Viola had returned to the trailer for coffee, she thought she heard or at least felt his presence in the back room. But Viola always acted as if they were alone.

Then one morning she arrived at the trailer to find a note pinned to the door saying that Viola was in town and that if she wanted, she could go in and make herself some coffee. Don't worry, you won't wake Chico.

But the second time she clanked the tin coffee pot onto the table she heard a stirring in the back of the trailer and, by the time she settled down to her cup, Chico appeared, water still dripping from his face, and with a clean T-shirt this time.

"Sorry, did I wake you? Viola left a note saying to come in and fix myself coffee. Like some? I've got a few granola bars too if that interests you. Usually Viola and I go for a desert walk in the mornings, but I guess she won't be back in time."

Lucy spoke rapidly, barely looking up.

Chico dropped wordlessly into the chair across from her and stared into the cup of bubbling black liquid she poured for him. One of his hands moved up to his face, sliding over his forehead and then covering his still closed eyes, as if to sooth them, or what lay behind, then fell heavily to the table. His eyes opened but seem to take a few moments to see Lucy.

"I could use a walk myself."

She followed him out the trailer, down a ravine and onto a path that took them between a pair of great rocks—erratics, mementos of the retreating glacier—then around a hill and into an area of flat crusty ground studded with simple concrete or wooden grave markers.

"Viola never took you here? Maybe it's too sad for her. These are all her people, the Hia-Ced. She used to come here with me when I was a kid, but I stayed aside, over there."

He nodded in the direction of a gnarled and spreading mesquite tree.

"She'd just sit in here, by some graves, and sing. At least I think she was singing—I'd hear a soft chanting or humming that seemed to come from her, but I don't think I ever knew for sure."

"So, you're not Hia-Ced? Her people, you said."

They had found seats on some large rocks on a small rise overlooking the cemetery, Lucy relaxing enough to look him in the eye as he spoke.

"No. My father was regular O'odham, you know? Tohono O'odham. A subtle distinction I guess for people from outside. Desert People—that's the Tohono O'odham; and Hia-Ced O'odham are Sand People. Same language just about—like you and I speak the same English, not quite, but we understand each other."

Chico laughed for the first time. Though he had seemed content to walk and talk with Lucy, whenever they were silent, he would drift away, his face tightening, and if they sat his hands would dig into the loose sand or fiddle with small stones as if driven to do so. Then he'd look up, as if remembering where he was, and with whom. But now his ebony eyes were alight and saw what was before them. He reached over to flick a beetle off her leg, letting his finger stay a tiny bit longer than necessary. The sun caught a few fine blonde hairs on her arm and lit up the honey-colored curls falling around her ears. Lucy felt his eyes along with the sun, both warming her skin. It was a feeling that would have sent her running in college, but here in her desert she felt no inclination to bolt, and the wounds he had revealed in their silences drew her to him.

"Your father?"

"Yeah, Carlos was his name. Didn't know him real well cause he packed up and slipped off into the night when I was a little kid. My mother raised me. Well, actually, Viola more did. Mom was kind of a nut, really. Christian nut, that is. Holy Roller, really busy with God and the Holy Spirit. Aunt Viola—that's what I always called her—took care of me, taught me about the desert, on walks like this one."

"So was your mother…"

"No, not Indian at all. A crazy Irish woman. I guess I've got a whole shitload of relations over there clinging to some rocky shore or other. When I was real young my mother still spoke of that world, the world of her father, but once she went Christian all that no longer mattered for her, no more than the Indian stuff here. And then she took me away from this, to the Reservation oddly enough. Only because that's where the church was."

Chico talked on, telling Lucy about his days on the T.O. Rez, running with the West Side Crips, then escaping the Rez and everything local.

"So why did you come back to Ajo?"

He didn't answer for a long moment.

"The Army kind of made sense for a while, at least it gave me a way to be … but then it didn't anymore … make sense."

Chico's eyes looked down and his hand played nervously in the sand. Lucy was going to ask him what he meant, but then thought better of it.

"So, I sort of drifted … I mean I came back and got some jobs, nothing really, and then I kind of ran out of everything—you know, money, friends, a point … I guess I lost my bearings, or maybe just came to the end of one road and needed to come back here to find another. Though I admit I haven't done much to locate it, sleeping too much and maybe drinking a little too much. Definitely drinking too much. The worst thing is that the Ajo folk think there's nothing wrong with any of that. And Viola's very patient."

He laughed at himself, rubbing his sandy hand on his jeans and looking into Lucy's gold green eyes.

"What about you? Are you a lifer in Fish and Game now? I think Viola is training you up to be the last Hia-Ced, walking the old desert paths."

"I don't know." She laughed softly. "It *is* a little strange. Like, the job is nothing much really. Just if I make it something." She looked about her at the sweep of the land and then directly into Chico's smiling eyes. "The desert is what's real for me. Does that make me one kind of O'odham or the other?" She laughed louder this time and touched Chico's hand, now hot from the morning sun.

They rose together and moved away from the graves, walking into a soft sand wash that ran under the sheltering shade of a cottonwood canopy. Lucy talked about her childhood, of how little she missed her family, and matched his stories with her own observations of her neighbors at Shady K and the parade of wilderness pilgrims and virile hunters that passed through the Refuge. The sun was now high in the sky, bearing down on the desert like an unforgiving father and they decided to wait out the hottest part of the day, reclining in the shade. Without a word, Chico took out a small joint from his shirt pocket and lit it. He inhaled deeply and passed it to Lucy, who drew a tentative breath before passing it back to him. Nearly asleep, Lucy reached over and let her fingers light on Chico's shoulder. His eyes were only half-opened as he pulled her to him. She let her lips graze and move along his, until she vanished, leaving only a tongue darting softly into the cave of his mouth. Then sleep.

The next morning when Lucy arrived for their walk, Viola had a different sort of desert place in mind.

"Follow me."

They made their difficult way south across the rock-strewn path that led up to Temporal Pass, encountering a stunning array of personal debris left by migrants on their way through in the other direction: tin cans, sleeping bags, bras, electrolyte bottles, jackets. Most things had been dropped or tossed along the way, but some articles of clothing were neatly folded, as if ready for a drawer. From the top of the pass, Viola and Lucy looked south across the grim creosote flatlands of the Growler Valley. Beyond it were the Agua Dulce hills and Mexico.

"Look down there."

Viola waved her hand slowly over the valley, where a fine lacework of soft-edged white paths cut through the green. All the paths were going south to north, several of them converging just below where the women stood.

"I knew there were a lot of illegal roads," Lucy said, "but seeing them from here…"

"That's right, honey. The people walking get dropped off down there. They climb up that steep trail and then across the pass toward my place. I see them go by most every night."

Viola then moved over to another ledge and, holding on to a stunted ironwood for support, leaned over and pointed directly below.

"But you see that wider road, the one that winds into the canyon? Months of heavy tires digging out moon dust sand. Now why do you suppose they'd be going that way? I know that place well. My poor husband, Morgan, used to run cattle there, had an old pump well and a charco—a watering pond for the livestock. But that's long since filled up with sand. There's only a few scraps of ruins left of the corral and such. Couldn't be people they are taking there, 'cause there's no way out except the way they're going in."

"Unless they are dropping something off and picking it up later?" Lucy asked. "Then driving on around to the loop road?"

Viola laughed, then, looking like she was on to more than the drug-runners, observed, "You're catchin' on to local ways, honey! Maybe we should get Chico and check it out."

* * *

Lucy had persuaded Viola to come along to her boss's public lecture, imagining that attendance might be poor. "Maybe bring Chico too?" She needn't have worried. The annual Refuge lecture was always assured a good turnout. Along with the loyal "snowbirds," there was always a crowd of belligerent locals expecting bad news on closures and looking forward to a good fight. A mix of ranchers, ex- and wannabe cowboys, vagabonds, hunters, and retirees, they were united by a common, near total, distaste for anything "federal." The government, at whose ample tit they had sucked for generations, was a distant evil, locally embodied in a gang of lazy liars conniving to thwart them in their honest efforts to make a living or have a good time.

The lights dimmed, and the first slide hit the screen: a delicate little ruminant poking its nervous tan and white face through a bunch of Gaeta Grass, a pink laser dot jumping about between the creature's neatly forked, forward-tilting horns. Standing next to the screen, the manager's skeletal form loomed ghoulish in the half-light, his Adam's apple, just visible, bobbled as he began to speak.

"Superficially similar to the American pronghorn, familiar in many parts of the West, your Sonoran pronghorn has adapted to the extremes of its desert habitat over many generations, in the process becoming different enough from their cousins farther north to be considered a subspecies, or even a species."

The door behind Lucy banged open and Kastenbader made his entry, falling heavily into a seat nearby and, so she thought, giving her, Viola, and Chico a quick and less than friendly glance.

The manager ambled through the fascinating past, precarious present, and uncertain future of the Sonoran pronghorn, illustrated by a series of blurry slides: presumed pronghorn caught by remote cameras; rainfall charts; densely lined maps of habitats and animal distribution; sunsets over the Pinta sands. Only the snowbirds pretended to listen, though the older men had started to drop off into snoring oblivion by the fifth slide.

The message, to which the speaker returned in his summing up, was the important difference between the little Sonoran and its relation, the America pronghorn, whose huge and healthy herds cavorted throughout the western prairies. Their Sonoran cousins, while adapting to the rigors of the desert, had developed differently and, in the end, fared far worse. Smaller and more delicate, they needed vast tracts of desert lands to sustain paltry numbers. But dammed rivers and new highways north and south of the border had sliced through their formerly vast territory, separating herds and leaving each with a smaller and less varied habitat.

The manager passed quickly through federal efforts to save the Sonoran pronghorn, first by designating it an endangered species. Then, by adding steadily to its protected domain, currently including all the Refuge, the Goldwater Bombing Range, and a good deal of BLM territory, much of which had been at one time leased to ranchers. It added up to a tract of land much bigger than the state of Connecticut, leaving only a few modest strips to the running of cattle or the joys of desert four-wheeling. He concluded with a description of efforts currently underway to save the tiny herd.

"We have helicoptered several pronghorn up from the Mexican herd and we'll be keeping them in an enclosure, where they'll breed, and then be periodically released into the Refuge, regenerating the local population."

The lights went on, a sickeningly bright fluorescent glare that startled the comatose and enlivened the restless. Time for questions.

Jake Evers rose, his work-gnarled hands—one clasped the chair before him and the other worked away at his chin—an unspoken indictment of soft government workers. He looked slowly about him before facing the manager, by way of indicating that he spoke for many.

"I don't know what flyin' pronghorn from Mexico cost us taxpayers, but I hear tell that all but two of 'em died on the way. I guess you science fellows have your own ways of doin' things, but killin' off your so-called endangered species strikes me as an odd way to go about savin' em."

Bitter laughter rippled through the room. The manager played nervously with the laser button. Evers continued.

"Why don't they just truck down some healthy bucks from Wyoming, and let them juice up this herd, hey?"

Clearly, Evers wasn't buying the "subspecies" argument. Like most of his neighbors, he saw the so-called *Sonorans* as simply a cornered, sickly herd of ordinary pronghorn, enfeebled through interbreeding, not unlike much of the local human population and about as deserving of special treatment. Encouraged by the audience reaction, he continued.

"And where they got the notion that takin' all the cattle away was gonna help the pronghorn ... Christ, everybody knows your pronghorn hops along with the cattle happy as the day is long. They feel safe with them, and they are too! Your coyote don't bother 'em any. And we'd clean out all the brush around the waterholes, and they'd like that too. Could see around then. Damn ecol-o-gists have got us run crazy. Now they won't let us clean up like that. Leave it more *natural*, they say. Hell, now it's *natural*, the pronghorn won't go near the water, 'cause they can't see what's hidin' in that damn *natural brush*. So, they're dyin' of thirst!"

Evers paused dramatically and then delivered the coup de grâce.

"Since you've been protectin' them, your so-called *Sonoran* pronghorn has gone from a few hundred to a few dozen. Down Mexico, you came up with some because they're still a few hundred head there. How come they're survivin'? Well, the cattle are out with 'em! And, back here, I know you're about to yank my damn lease!"

Evers sat down to loud applause. The manager decided on a meek smile. No need to answer. After all, there wasn't really a question. Most of the snowbirds, volunteers at the Refuge, were uncomfortably confused. But the locals were firmly behind Evers. Few were ranchers, but the others were still Westerners, and as such believed that all government agencies and employees were at the very least incompetent, if not evil. Besides, the only real pleasure afforded by the wild landscape in which they lived was churning through it at high speed and volume on their all-terrain vehicles—a joy threatened by those damned pronghorn.

Seeing an opportunity to ride in with the ranchers, Clyde rose to the occasion.

"I'm like Jake here. And as a businessman, I am wondering whether your money was well spent on helicopters. Hell man, if you needed Mexican pronghorns, I know the territory down there and I'd a got me some of my boys, gone down and rounded 'em up for you. Drove 'em here like cattle, on horseback, right up into the Refuge."

As usual, Clyde was talking only for effect, but by the time he had finished he had come to believe his own ravings. He smiled broadly at the laughter, which he figured was at the manager's expense. Until he caught Evers leaning over to say something to another rancher:

"That drug-running bastard couldn't round up a fence post."

Kastenbader pulled his Texas brim down over a reddening face, doing his best to pretend he hadn't heard. The floor was quickly taken by an aging salesclerk whose knowledge of the world of ranching and cowboys was pretty much confined to what he could glean from watching the Sunday afternoon roping in Sanchez' back lot. He rose to his booted feet to lament any farther losses of cattle leases, speaking of the tragic demise of a way of life, a culture….

He was interrupted by a resonant baritone booming from the back of the meeting room.

"The Nazis had a culture too. Doesn't mean it needed preserving!"

Shocked silence, as all heads swiveled around, fixing on a tall, swarthy man standing at the very rear of the room with a fanatically calm grin on his face. Eco-nuts (as the locals knew them) didn't usually have the balls to show up at meetings in Ajo.

The room exploded into growls and shouts. But the stranger remained impassive until the uproar had run its course, and then added.

"Cattle are the worst enemy the West ever had, and the land will begin to recover only when every last one of them is taken off."

When he had finished his piece, he slipped out the way he came in amid ugly stares and muttered threats. Kastenbader followed him, to the puzzled looks of his neighbors. He was back inside a moment later, where the still shocked and angry crowd was gathered in complaining groups.

"Told him where to get off!" he crowed.

What he did was get the man's phone number.

The food at Margarita's has certainly put Evi in a better mood. He shakes his head in disbelief at Clyde's plan, but can't help smiling as he plucks another *gordita* laden with tender, smoky barbacoa into his mouth.

Clyde is almost too happy to eat.

"Those little animals are gonna solve all our *problemas, hermano*. The faunin' season is startin' in a few weeks, so the pronghorn are on everyone's mind, but just to be sure I've got that eco guy from Tucson comin' out to do a field trip right in the old ranchin' area that we're usin' for the drops. Got a bunch of old farts from Shady K goin' out with him, and I should be able to get someone from the Refuge. Maybe the manager himself. I'll tell him it would be a nice gesture for the snowbird volunteers, plus he knows the eco guy is gonna come down hard on cattle. And, right when he's in the middle of his lecture on the evils of ranchin', three of his precious Sonoran pronghorn are gonna go prancin' by. Witnessed by everybody. And that will seal the fuckin' deal, *hermano*. They'll have to close down the whole area, shoehorn the crazy old Indian out of her shit-box trailer; pull Evers' lease for fuckin' ever. Nobody will be out there but us."

Evi takes another big bite, talking while he chews.

"They'll do all that for a few antelope? And how do you know they're going to show up like that?"

Clyde swirls a rolled tortilla in his *refrijitos*, trails it through the bowl of salsa and stuffs the dripping mess into his reddened and sweating face, now twisting into a coy smile. He brays through a full mouth,

"Guess you don't know what a great country you're dealin' with. One of those babies is enough to scrub a fuckin' bombin' run out there on the Air Force Range. And as far as the pronghorn showin' up on cue, that, *hermano*, is well in hand."

Leaning over the salsa with uncontained excitement, Clyde tells Evi how he has gotten the boys in Las Mesitas to drop a net over a few pronghorn down in the Mexican herd—illustrating by letting a tortilla drop like a turd from his pudgy paw, onto the saltshaker. "A modest *mordita* to your local authorities and in they went with a truckload of inspected cattle. Sailed across the border, no fuckin' problem, *hermano*. Got them safe in one of my sheds right up in Ajo, ready for their moment of glory."

"'Couldn't round up a fence post?' Fucking Evers." Clyde chortles to himself as Evi hefts another wad of *barbacoa* homeward.

* * *

Meanwhile, Divina Luz is attending to more mundane matters up in Ajo: sorting food stamps in the back room of the Circle K while keeping one eye trained on the front counter, where Lupe is slumped in her habitual attitude of complacent ennui. It's the kind of pose that always sends Clyde into paroxysms. Not Divina Luz. Even if she puts the stick to Lupe now and again, she does not really mind an indolence which she understands to be inextricably linked to beauty and desirability and leading to the right sort of marriage. But her reveries are rudely interrupted by the familiar rasping sputter of an Oldsmobile pulling up to the store.

Chico waits outside while Viola bustles into the Circle K. She has made him stop so that she could pick up a few things, but to judge by how little time she spends looking at the shelves and how much more leaning over the counter talking to Lupe, now joined by Divina Luz, he figures it was information she was after.

Wily old woman smells something, but for once she's got it wrong. Yeah, he has gone out with Lupe a few times and yeah, she is way too young for him, maybe even too wild, and of course her father is the biggest asshole in Ajo. But it hasn't come to anything.

The last time they were together was just after the desert walk with Lucy. Chico went into the Circle K that night to pick up a six pack and found Lupe behind the counter, with a short halter top exposing her belly and the silver chain dangling from a pierced navel. She caught him staring and asked if he wanted to get high on something stronger than beer, and while he considered the offer, she turned the open sign on the door around and led him out of the shop and into the parking lot. He followed her out to the edge of town, where the desert lots were larger, and a variety of home-made tin sheds housed everything from crippled trailers to animal feed. Several of these were Kastenbader's, he knew, his old hauling business occupied one and in others he stored supplies for his many Ajo enterprises. They arrived at one, before which heaps of scrap metal glinted in the moonlight. Inside, she led him by the hand around stacked hay bales and then on around to the back of the shed. "Look," she said, her face glowing crazy in the flashlight, and scraping off a layer of straw on what had seemed an ordinary bale, she revealed a huge block of tightly packed marijuana.

"All these in the back are dope, man! I knew my father was up to something, and so I snooped around with my dog till I found these. You don't think anyone will miss a joint or two's worth from one of these?"

They smoked alright, but when he began to kiss her, his hand tracing the silver chain, he couldn't get Lucy's sleepy desert face out of his mind. The taste of her lips.

The car door creaks open.

"I don't like it."

Viola climbs back in beside Chico, treating him to a cold-eyed stare.

"Your little girlfriend's father is up to something, but I haven't figured out yet what it is. It's him behind that nature nut everybody was screaming about after last week's lecture. He's got him coming out to Morgan's old well tomorrow morning. Everybody's invited. Now, we know that somebody has been stashing dope down there. And of all the likely suspects, that son-of-a-bitch Kastenbader is at the top of the list, so why would he want everybody to go down there?"

Chico has no idea, in fact, but is for the moment relieved that Viola has not grilled him about Lupe, or about Lucy—whom he met earlier that evening. Of course, Viola would be delighted to know that Lucy is on his mind now, but he doesn't want to give her the satisfaction of getting her way or feel the pressure of her approval.

Chico and Lucy had walked the length of the town and beyond, the moonlight illuminating their path through the desert sands. They said little, Lucy looking sideways at Chico, at the easy strength of his stride and then at his ambiguous face. Was he calmly contemplative or just lost? In fact, Chico wasn't sure himself. He felt a sense of movement with Lucy, a possible breaking of the walking trance in which he had been living since coming back to Ajo. But was he moving forward, or back? A question made concrete by his immediate destination. He was taking Lucy to Kastenbader's shed—the strategy of a teenager. But living in Viola's trailer had given him the options of a teenager, and, he had to admit, the bed of straw and the joint he would roll with the paper in his pocket were as appealing as they would be to any eighteen-year-old. He found the key where Lupe had put it, in the freezer compartment of the defunct fridge leaning against the shed, and brought Lucy into the sweet-smelling chamber, lit by the stripes of moonlight that found their way between the corrugated panels.

* * *

It is nearly dawn and Clyde is already in place down at the well, anxiously awaiting the imminent delivery of his surprise guests to the makeshift little corral hidden behind an adobe wall. The truck should be on its way from town, so everything will be in place for the moment when, with Mr. Kill-the-Cowboy hammering away before his attentive audience later that morning, Clyde will signal, the corral door will swing open, and the little *Mexicanas*, as he has been calling the smuggled pronghorns, will prance right by the assembly.

But the truck is not on the way.

The driver has, in fact, pulled up to Kastenbader's storage shed. But he finds no key on the ledge, and the door's locked from the inside. He is about to force the door when he hears voices inside. Wrong shed, he thinks, remounting the truck and rumbling through the dark in search of another.

"Hey, I think I hear a truck outside. No, it's going away now," Viola whispers, then motions to Lucy, who has reluctantly followed her on this predawn raid. She told Viola about the shed, leaving Chico out of the story, and of course she wanted to see for herself.

A thin shaft of dawn light from a crack between sheets of the tin roof illuminates Viola's bent form. She has peeled back the canvas on a pallet of bales and is poking a long finger into one of them.

"Here's his stash, just scratch away some of this hay…".

But Lucy is busy in another dimly lit corner. Chuckling softly, her head is thrust under a canvas she has lifted from another crate.

"More dope? Viola queries.

"Not exactly," Lucy replies.

A soft clatter of scraping hoofs echoes through the chamber.

* * *

The manager's white pickup bounces into the clearing around Morgan's well, carrying the eco guy and trailed by a convoy of shiny SUVs piloted by Shady K-ers, who disembark, excited for any event that punctuates their winter. Jake Evers, having received a call from his cousin that made his day, is sitting comfortably in his truck, watching Kastenbader stare dumbly into the distance, kicking chunks of clay off a nearby adobe ruin.

The guest speaker climbs up onto the manager's lowered truck tailgate ready to begin his condemnation of the iniquities of ranching, and the Shady K-ers in their floppy brim hats, crowd around to hear. But before he can do more than clear his throat, he is engulfed in the swirling cloud of powdery dust kicked up by Evi's truck, which has finally arrived. Kastenbader rushes, cursing, toward the vehicle, but jerks to a halt when he realizes that the driver is in uniform. Evi's man is slunk down in the back seat of one of the two Border Patrol vehicles that follow the truck into the clearing, followed in turn by a Refuge Jeep carrying Lucy, Viola, and Chico.

The whole parade comes to a raucous halt before the suddenly silent crowd, joined now by Evers. They have forgotten the speaker, still standing dumbly on the tailgate, and have turned to face the new drama. From within the billowing yellow dust, they can hear Kastenbader's eerie whine and the loud clatter of hoofs echoing inside the truck.

The Border Patrol agents, conscious of the publicity of their performance, fairly bounce out of their car. One of them has Evi's driver by the arm, like a naughty child, pulling him to the front of the assembly. The prisoner, who has clearly and wisely weighed his options, nods reluctantly toward the stupefied Kastenbader, who groans as he sinks to his quaking knees, his eagle-feathered hat sliding forward over his face. Pulling out cuffs and guns, the agents head toward him, visibly delighted by this departure from the routine business of chase and arrest.

6

Burying Sheila Cassidy

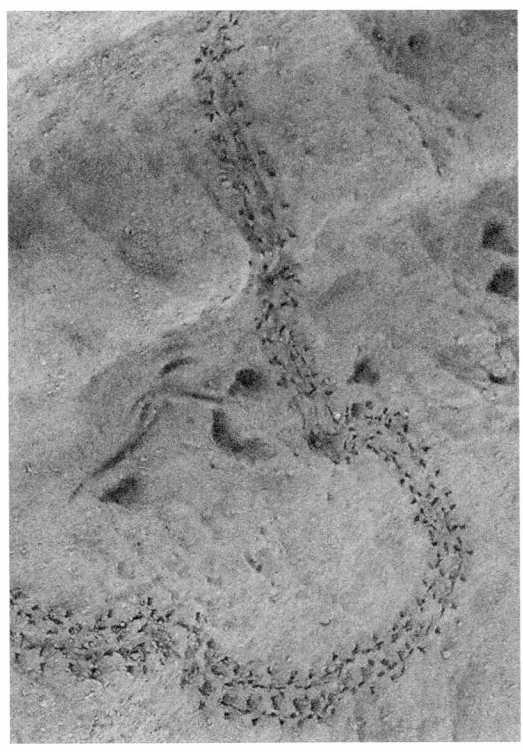

Fig. 6.1 Photograph by Maeve Hickey

© The Author(s) 2020
L. J. Taylor, *Tales from the Desert Borderland*, Palgrave Studies in Literary Anthropology, https://doi.org/10.1007/978-3-030-35133-5_6

Chico awakens to the whirr of crow wings flapped once in a glide, black shadows circling on blacker gravel. Rising stiffly on one elbow, he turns to see Angelina's shock of ebony hair, a brushstroke above her sleeping bag. A feeble warmth clings to the remains of the fire and cactus wrens are rummaging through the charred sticks and ashes, poking at hidden bugs. Cartoon-quick, a squirrel creeps down to the edge of the camp, only to twist around and scamper straight up the rocks to his hidden burrow. Everything is in its burrow. The floor of the desert broken by a thousand holes: the size of an acorn, the size of a fist, the size of a football. On the surface nothing stirs. But delicate prints reveal the business of the night, a restless traffic of cats crisscrossing every open space.

They walk again. In the now dead, bird-less air, they hear only the crunch of their boots and the soft pulse of their own blood as they plod up the loose gravel and then, coming over a ridge, descend into a vale of red earth and softer, more luxuriant foliage. Nearly iridescent green *palo verde* trees embrace majestic saguaro or spreading organ pipes. Between are ocotillos: stark but verdant in life, grayly strange in death. Fallen over, their flesh turns a fuzzy mold and flakes off like ashes, leaving a graceful lattice skeleton on the desert floor. One, whose many long thin arms have splayed when they hit the ground, suggests the poignant remains of a giant squid sunk to the bottom of a now waterless sea.

Angelina has curled up under a mesquite tree. Chico sits nearby and closes his eyes. He will rest for only a moment before moving on again. They need to reach the cave by nightfall. But sleep comes.

The deep green waters of the sea drain from the skies, leaving him standing naked, wet and cool on the dimly lit carpet of black rocks. He follows the retreating water between the boulders, arriving at a small pool. Leaning over, he sees his reflection, at once younger and older than himself. That image fades, replaced by the fleeting glimpse of the flipper. A sea turtle, whose eye rises for one hypnotic second to catch him in its glassy stare. Without speaking, the turtle says, "I was here first, before the land had taken form. Who are you? Stranger or kin?"

This journey began in Sells, capital of the *Tohono* O'odham Nation.

Chico pulled up to the *Indian Café* and coaxed the ancient Olds into a space between a shiny new van with blackened windows and an old pickup with the words *Comes 'round again* in bold script across the doors. Dilapidated wooden fencing bolted to the truck bed extended the cargo space upward, where fraying ropes secured a stacked tower of battered and stained furniture. Anywhere else that shit would be on its way out. All these years, nothing has changed.

Inside, two tables were full. Five young O'odham men leaned over what looked like the café's entire daily supply of French fries: teetering greasy heaps glowing with crimson ketchup. Chico could feel their eyes on his dusty boots and tired jeans. On his whiteness. The other table was all uniforms. Three Reservation police: one Indian and two white guys lifting mugs of coffee and looking up as he passed. Hesitating between a reflexive salute and the deeper, Rez habit of looking down in the presence of lawmen, he managed a half nod. But officers come and go and there was no one to remember some nameless gang kid from twenty-some years before.

He found a corner seat across from a community bulletin board blanketed with curling printouts. *Apostolic camp coming up soon. AA meeting at Santa Rosa. Rodeo Queen pageant.* But most were notices of death. Ricky Lopez, a hulking eighteen-year-old, grins over his snare drum set (a stabbing death of two days before). Young Lois Baraceda smiles sweetly (too dazed by beer and pot to see the car sailing toward her through the starry night). Carlito, a thin young man of twenty-two, appears calmly reflective (found hanging in his grandmother's garage). Beverly Wilson. Heavy, sixties maybe, frilled collared dress, saintly smile (diabetes). And below Beverly, the unusually delicate figure of a woman with a small white face capped by a bowl of gray blonde hair: Sheila Cassidy.

For one long, strange moment Chico stared into the shadowy printer dot eyes, feeling no surprise, only recognition of the woman whose possible death he had been contemplating since her letter arrived some days before.

A soft, warm hand moved up and down his forearm and he turned to see Janet, clutching a steaming carafe of coffee: Our Lady of Indian Consolation.

"Thought you might come home. Sorry, Chico."

She poured him a cup of coffee as he slumped back into his chair.

"Can I get you anything else?" Her face was as round and reassuring as the moon.

He shook his head and took the letter out of his pocket, as if by reading the words of his living mother, her death might be rendered less abrupt, slowed into a space he could still enter. There were few words, and while Sheila was always given to elliptical remarks, they usually contained some reference to Jesus or the Holy Ghost. The letter, however, spoke of other deities:

Son,
The Ocean has cursed me.
You must come and help me. Come right away.
The Ocean is killing me.

* * *

Chico's childhood with his mother had not featured the Ocean at all, much less as some kind of deity. His earliest years were spent in Ajo, a bleak mining town deep in the desert beyond the Rez, whose shack homes clustered around the open mine pit in concentric rings, like the circles of Hell. Furthest from the pit were the houses of the Whites, closer in were the Mexicans. And finally, clinging to the very edge of the ever-widening maw was "Indiantown." His father, Carlos, had taken one of those precarious cabins when he returned from his second tour in Vietnam. Nothing unusual in that. Many Indians had come back to find no work on the Rez and wanted more than running a few stringy cattle could offer. The mines were humming, and the money seemed good. That is, before the rent and company store groceries were deducted from the packet. But his mother's path was twisty from the start. She was the daughter of Irishman Francis Cassidy, who had left the craggy shores of Donegal for the promise of California only to drift from mine to mine, from the Anaconda strikes up in Montana to the deep shafts of Colorado to the open copper pits here in southern Arizona. Each move had wearied his body and lowered his prospects, but they were never so low that he imagined his daughter—even with a mother dead before the girl had reached ten—would take up with an Indian. But she did, and in her nineteenth year found herself pregnant and disowned by a father whose whiteness was the only thing left to him. Sheila moved into Carlos's shack, and he settled into work at the mine.

This arrangement was as much a surprise to the Indians as it was to the Whites. Not that there was no mixing, but it was always the other way 'round: a white father knocking up some Indian girl and leaving the progeny to join his or her less fortunate maternal relations. There was no marriage between Sheila and Carlos either and their boy kept his mother's name. He was Francis, like her father, but Francisco to the Mexicans and Indians—Chico for short. And there were years enough of housekeeping to bring mother and child into the Indian fold. When Carlos began to head off on his solo journeys and finally left the mines and his little family for good, Aunt Viola, a widowed neighbor, moved in with them and was seen to be the real head of the household. Sheila was just another lost, half-breed kid. Along with little Chico, who followed his mother, his eyes on the stars, on her wandering walks away from everything.

But never to the ocean.

* * *

Chico left the café and spent the rest of the morning driving around Sells, resisting the first beer till a bit after ten, suddenly aware of what his aunt Viola called his "raggedy-ass" condition: barely washed, soiled jeans, and shapeless black T-shirt. Even for him, this quest was especially erratic. He had come without thought or preparation, saying nothing to Lucy—indeed, putting her out of his thoughts entirely until that moment. And he hadn't dressed to see his mother alive, much less at her wake. With his left hand lightly on the wheel and his right popping open and lifting cans, he coasted past the old haunts—VFW hall, still advertising the Friday night fish fry; town library, door barred by a hobbled pony rolling in the dust—and pulled up to a small, white clapboard church. Assembly of God.

Comforted by the first tinge of beery dizziness in the growing heat, he stood staring at the church and then walked around behind the building where the silent members of the "Assembly" lay beneath a huddle of hand-wrought crosses and tablets.

* * *

They were on one of their wandering walks through a summer night beyond the mine and shacks when Sheila said, "Listen." Music. Though it might have been coyotes or the wind. They walked toward the sound, his mother moving like a charmed creature. Witched. And little Chico floated behind her, as if she were gently pulling him through the water or the sky. Because at night the sky over the desert can be like water. You are weightless, always rising as if you were walking on the bottom of the sea. So, they had gone along that way, toward the music. Voices in the night sky, drawing them in.

The canvas, white as moonlight, held aloft by poles, was rippled by the breezes into soft waves. Beneath it, people sat in rows of folding chairs surrounded by hundreds of tall candles, their flames like stars that had fallen and gathered around them. The congregation was singing. Woeful, beautiful, Indian-softened, Christian hymns. Chico followed his mother through this circle of light that threw the world behind them into deeper darkness, and, looking up, saw her stricken face in the eerily flickering glow. Then suddenly there were two women, big as houses, taking his mother by her arms, smiling, saying "Come sister, come to the Lord." He followed as they led her up the center aisle. All the heads turned to see them as they walked to the preacher, the biggest white man Chico had ever seen. He reached out, taking hold of Sheila's head as you would a fragile egg, and said, "Pray with me." She fell to her knees and more ladies gathered around her. Kneeling, each put one hand on his mother's bent, shaking back, and raised the other up to the sky. And so, she was a Christian. Well, they baptized her later on, and Chico too, but it didn't change him, and she was already changed, already "an Assembly."

The big white man was the regular Assembly preacher over on the Rez, in Sells, where there was a much larger and holier congregation than the little group in Ajo whose Sunday meetings were held in a tin shed: the noise of the fans drowned out even the Holy Spirit when He was speaking through some ecstatic lady. Sometimes his mother would get them a ride out to Sells, an hour or so bouncing in the back of a pickup, and they would attend the service there in a proper wooden chapel with white clapboard and windows.

One Sunday, a new, O'odham, preacher, gave a sermon Chico would always remember. He started off talking about the beautiful baskets the People made: tight enough to hold water. Chico had a cousin José who wove them, a lovely fat man with great sausage fingers you couldn't imagine working the delicate bear grass and reeds. The preacher spoke of the loving care of the weaver, the basket-maker, who turned out to be God, weaving the world, weaving their lives. God up there, like a big fat Indian, like cousin José, holding reeds and grass between his thick fingers. The preacher said that the Indians who made baskets were doing something wonderful and sacred, and Chico was so proud of his cousin, of all the O'odham.

But then, suddenly, the picture changed, and the preacher was furious, warning them that some of those basket-makers were in "the gravest danger of Hell." Chico didn't know how they had gotten so quickly from Heaven to Hell, but the preacher made it clear. The design the weavers put on their baskets was the problem: a maze of circles with a figure at the outer opening: *I'itoi*. Creator. Elder Brother. The guide through that maze. Evil, the preacher said. Devil worship that would—he roared this out at them—land them all in Hell. So, what had started out making them all happy and proud now scared them all—and not just the kids like Chico. He could still remember the faces of the adults, including his mother. They were all frightened. Worse, they were ashamed. Like they had been very bad children caught out by a mean father. Then the preacher told them what to do. They were to go to their homes and gather up baskets, pictures, anything with *I'itoi* on it, put it all in a sack or box and bring it back to the church the next Sunday.

So that's what they did. Sheila dedicated herself to cleaning up their house, their lives, of Evil. When they arrived in Sells the next Sunday, they heard the congregation singing, outside, behind the church, where they formed a circle around a great heap of sacks and boxes bulging and brimming over with Evil. Burning. The flames were whipping at the sky and the air was wild with the heat, little pieces of dried baskets or paper popping and rising with the flames. His mother ran toward the inferno, her sack dragging from one hand and Chico from the other. The circle opened to let them through, and they went up to the fire, and together added their sack to the flames, the wall of intense heat slapping their faces.

* * *

Chico stood staring at the church, smaller than he remembered, and then checked his mother's death notice for the time and place of the wake in the flowing script at the bottom: *Consuela Antone. Saguaro Way.* Her three-bed HUD box sat in the dirt just beyond the Assembly graveyard.

But Chico found no wake, only Consuela in her barren living room, conferring with a very large man in horn-rimmed glasses. Seeing Chico, she bounded up from the sofa and greeted him with an unfamiliar, effusive, tear-streaked warmth. Then the man rose and moved toward them with a self-important step, shifting his bulk from one leg to the other.

"I am Pastor Williams. Your mother," he said in simple but emphatic tones, "is in mortal danger."

Although an Indian, his voice had exactly the inflection of the White Assembly preacher of years before.

Chico stared dumbly.

"Danger?"

"Her soul."

The Pastor's round and deep brown face, covered in a perfect sheen of perspiration, hung immobile inches from Chico's.

"Your father's sisters took your mother away from Consuela's tender care." He turned for a moment toward the now inconsolably sobbing Consuela. "The care of all of us in the Assembly of God."

"The Catholics came and took her to Topowa!" Consuela put it more simply.

He imagined the scene: his father's ardent Catholic sisters hijacking Sheila's living, feverish, pain-wracked body. God knows they cared little enough for his poor mother while she was alive, so they must have been trying to capture her in time to preside over her death. And then bury her alongside the husband she had not seen for decades. Among the Catholics.

"The poor woman was besieged by the devil."

Pastor Williams howled, all the while gripping Chico's forearm in his enormous fist.

"She was raving when she was ill, saying crazy things about the Ocean, and I had been preparing a cleansing prayer vigil only to find your aunts had taken her away. Now she has died in that awful, tormented state."

And those women have surely surrounded her with Roman confusion and perdition! Idolatry! They are determined to have the wake there. They have sent their minions round door to door this morning, inviting all to their house. You must go, Chico, and get your mother back here, back home with us!"

He let his great paw fall heavily on Chico's shoulder, gripping him like some fathers do their young sons, as if to inspire both affection and fear, nearly propelling him out the door on his Christian mission.

But once outside, Chico's gaze fell once again on the sorry gravestones, bathed in the merciless noon light. The unfocused regret he had been feeling about Sheila, about it being too late to find anything he had lost, slid beneath a simple, powerful determination to keep her out of this sad place. So, with that sense of limited, but more appealing, mission he drove south, down a road periodically crossed by tire marks left by drunks skidding into the brush to avoid the cows; hapless creatures who found their wandering way into the middle of the highways every night.

* * *

The morning had been quieter down in Topowa, a much smaller place than Sells, and nine miles closer to the Mexican border. The first light brought the sounds of cows knocking through the brushy mesquite, a stalled truck sputtering to a start, and a dozen migrants coughing and whispering as they rolled up their bedding in the sunken trough behind Jimmy Velasquez's house, while Jimmy used his cell phone to find out why his brother was late for the pickup.

Angelina, who had come home late the night before and had been asleep on the sofa, was startled from a hip-hop dream by the echoing scrape of metal folding chairs on the concrete floor. Her grandmother, Juana, was setting up for the wake.

"Christ, it isn't for hours. Why does she have to do this now? Just to destroy my sleep?"

Angelina said this out loud, as if she were addressing somebody, and then stretched one round arm out from under the blankets and tipped her bedside clock into view.

"Eight fucking thirty!"

She staggered into the bathroom where two other young brothers were retrieving toys left in the scummy bathtub the night before. She pushed them out and rummaged through a shoebox full of cosmetics for something that would say sexy but say it softly enough that her grandmother wouldn't hear. By ten o'clock she was ready for the day, squeezed into snow wash jeans and a billowing black T-shirt. She popped in a pair of scintillating green contact lenses, stuffed a neatly folded red bandanna into her back pocket, took one full turn before the mirror, and was out the door. Safely around the corner, Angelina inserted her iPod ear buds and was about to tie her colors around her neck when she saw her grandmother, Juana, with a stack of full Tupperware containers bearing down on her like a combine harvester.

"Where you goin'? You turn yourself around and get back to the house. You are gonna help me right here today. We're having a wake."

* * *

Chico arrived to find Juana blocking the doorway of her house like the meanest of bar bouncers.

"Chico." A statement, and implied question, not about identity, but intention. Was he there to cause trouble? There was no kinship in her hard eyes, not even the disappointment an aunt might feel looking at a wayward nephew who has dragged his, half-drunken, slothful body home too late. There was only a warning. His mother or not, he had no say in this home.

Reassured by a vacancy in his eyes that she took for defeat, Juana stepped aside to let Chico enter the living room—now transformed into a mini-chapel with rows of metal folding chairs, each emblazoned with the name of the favorite local beer, "*Tecate*," facing a large table supporting an open coffin. He passed down the aisle between two phalanxes of seated women. None of these would have been a friend to his mother. They were the town's leading Catholics, the ones who ran the show as weak-willed outsider priests came and went. Father Gilmartin, the incumbent, was there smiling meekly and nodding to Chico, while beside him, Chico's other aunt, Carmen, stood glowering with barely contained hostility. Coiffed heads pivoted to watch, approving but cautious, as Chico made his hesitant way toward his mother's open coffin.

Sheila looked disconcertingly alive and, unexpectedly, Irish. Rather like a mother pretending to sleep so that her children will leave her in peace. But she was surrounded by the very perdition the Assembly Pastor Williams feared: a chaos of candles in glasses adorned with polychrome etchings of *Nuestro Señor*, a table crowded with holy pictures and statues draped with colored ribbons, a lurid new Our Lady of Guadalupe, a careworn *Santo Niño de Atocha* missing much of his nose, and San Francisco Xavier, that stern, black-bearded, and robed sixteenth-century Basque Jesuit recumbent in his glass coffin. There was hardly an O'odham Catholic home without one. He came in all sizes: a tinker toy miniature is handy for the children; Grandma might want a foot-long version for her dresser-top; "life size" for the village shrine, like the one there, echoing his mother's open coffin.

Chico felt no more comforted by Roman theatrics than Assembly hysterics and was once again losing any sense that he should or could do anything for his mother. He found a seat near the back door, as if unrelated to the deceased, and let the odors of damp concrete and perfumed wax induce a beery, open-eyed, sickly sleep. He didn't notice Angelina taking a seat alongside him and was startled to feel a hand softly laid on top of his own. He turned to see the pretty teen, smiling at him with unlikely green eyes.

"Hi. I'm your cousin, Angelina. Juana's my gram. You're Chico, right? The old ladies were all whispering your name when you came in. Kind of fucked up, huh? Oh, sorry about your mom."

Chico's answer was interrupted by the crashing thud of the door, thrown open hard enough to bounce off the wall, nearly knocking him from his seat. The roused congregation turned as one to see Pastor Williams, large and furious as a Samoan wrestler. On either side of the intruder was a hefty Assembly women retainer—a daunting war party.

The Pastor, now commanding the room, took one dramatic stride inward and whipped off his glasses as if he were unleashing the malignant superpower of his eyes. One focused like a laser on the coffin. The other, apparently only intermittently under his control, screeed wildly about the room, alighting for a second here and there on startled Catholic faces.

"Your graven images will bring seven plagues down on your sinning heads!"

The Pastor pronounced these words in a biblical baritone, his colossal head swiveling slowly from side to side, taking in the now uniformly stunned audience, open mouthed and riveted to their *Tecate* seats. He paused to savor his mastery of the moment and then, suddenly, raised his arm up in a wide arc, gesturing imperiously toward the front of the room, as if to make the clutch of Catholic ladies sitting or standing between him and poor Sheila part like the Red Sea. His booming voice, now indisputably prophetic, filling the room.

"Our sister! Come away out of that demonic horror!"

Taking their cue, the two Assembly women hurled themselves headlong up the aisle, flowing like liquid vengeance toward the coffin, sending a few slow-moving, frightened Catholics spinning out of their path. Father Gilmartin effected the quivering retreat of a wounded rabbit and the entire congregation froze in stunned silence. But Juana and Carmen, who alone had risen to their steady feet at the Pastor's entrance, watching and waiting, unfazed, through his performance, moved to defend their sister-in-law in death as they never would have in life, stepping out in front of the coffin to form a massive, self-righteous wall of flesh between the deceased and the intruders.

The Assembly ladies were unprepared for resistance and ground to a noisy halt before the sisters. After a few moments of shrill, damning gospel citations, they could do nothing but slowly withdraw. Pastor Williams was left alone to face Juana and Carmen, who deadpanned in the ancient O'odham way, a ten-thousand-year-old stare right through their now unhinged enemy. He continued to spout assurances of divine retribution, but with decreasing confidence, all the time retreating and finally, as smoothly as it is possible for a man of that size, backing out the door. The words "justice" and "immortal soul" hung in the air behind him, but the sisters were left in undisputed ownership of poor Sheila. Father Gilmartin emerged from hiding to occupy, however tentatively, the clerical space, and Juana and Carmen returned to their seats with unseemly smirks of victory, Juana thrubbing a fat finger on the edge of the coffin on her way.

Chico and Angelina sought the open air, finding a few empty chairs just outside the door.

"Close one, huh, Chico? That's one for the Catholics!"

Her round, butternut face was enlivened with a sardonic grin.

"You know, my grandmother and all her friends, man. They're *happy* as shit to have Sheila back to bury her alongside their brother, your dad … that's *if* he's really there!"

Chico looked long and deep at his newly discovered cousin. He was still feeling mainly numb about his mother and he had frankly never given any thought to where his father was buried. But the possibility that his aunts had been in some way fooled was certainly appealing.

"What do you mean?"

"Uncle Nestor said something once … you know he hates my Gran and Aunt Carmen."

Nestor, his father's brother, was for Chico only a shadowy figure who came to visit them from his rancho down over the Mexican border, just before Chico's father left for good. A deep-chested man in a red flannel shirt, saying little, but listening to his father, whose voice was a low, plaintive murmur in the night.

Angelina, happy to have Chico's attention, continued.

"You know Nestor never comes up here? Well, one time, he did come, for a wake or something, and Gram said something nasty to him, like 'only death brings you up here. But once it's over, it's over for you, 'cause you never come up and lay flowers on your poor brother's grave.' Nestor didn't even look angry or upset. He just smiled and looked at her like she's a poor fool. 'I never neglect the dead,' he said, 'but you never did have any sense of where poor Carlos was at.' Well, Gran just acts, like, he's stupid—but I remember Uncle Nestor was always real smart, so I started thinkin' about what he said. I figure he meant that Uncle Carlos wasn't where Gran thought he was. Somehow Nestor took him off, probably down over the line."

Chico was about to ask for details when Angelina stood up to point out the powder blue 1958 Dodge truck that had rolled to a stop a bit farther along the road.

"That's him!"

* * *

Uncle Nestor remained in his truck as if he had done his duty just by showing up and wasn't about to enter Juana's house. He lit up a Camel and puffed with quiet determination, scowling like a beleaguered husband waiting for his wife in a Wal-Mart parking lot.

"Hello, Uncle Nestor. It's me, Chico. Carlos's son."

"I know who you are."

Nestor moved his head only slightly, giving Chico a side look that went right through his unshaven face, making him feel like a child and dissipating the comforting beer cloud in which he had been floating. Chico was about to ask about his father, but Nestor cut him off.

"I buried your father in Pozo Verde, where he belongs."

He paused, then added, looking directly at Chico for the first time.

"You should come down visit him one time."

The truck door swung open. Nestor had no legs. Diabetes, Chico understood. His uncle nodded toward the back of the truck where Chico found a folded-up wheelchair. Once it was set up, Nestor slid down into it with powerful precision. Chico and Angelina squatted on either side of the old man, as if to block any retreat, while Nestor leaned forward slightly, shifting his great, legless body in the wheelchair, looking defiant. There was more to the story, but he wasn't saying another word, at least for the moment.

But Angelina was determined to get him to talk. Chico watched her, unable to decide whether her green eyes, caught in the streetlight now, made her intriguing or just strange.

"Oh, come on, Uncle Nestor. I saw Uncle Carlos go into his grave. I was only a little girl, but I remember the funeral. And Gran and Aunt Carmen and all of them there watchin'!"

"You saw something go into the grave alright…"

He couldn't resist a knowing grin.

"You mean to say that wasn't Uncle Carlos? How did you get him out of the coffin?"

"Let's just say that there come a time when Carlos was all alone at the wake. Your mother and aunt left, and old Jorge came in to close up the coffin. Only Jorge was a friend of mine, and of Carlos too. Not hard to change that coffin for one with enough rocks to feel right."

"So, you smuggled him out?" Chico asked, finding himself excited at the idea.

"I took him down to Pozo Verde and buried him in the old way, with the old ones. I will take you to him when your mother is buried up here."

"I don't want her buried up here. I want to take her down to my father. Bury her there."

Chico said this without thinking, now determined to get his mother away from Juana and Carmen as much as from the Assemblies. Thinking of his mother's death reminded him of her letter, which he handed over to Nestor. The older man read it, saying nothing; only nodding, as if the words made sense.

* * *

Late Saturday morning at the Catholic cemetery. Chico's head was throbbing, and his neck ached from the few hours of sleep in the Olds, but he didn't try to wash the pain away with another beer. He stood decorously with his cousin. It was difficult for Angelina to come up with clothes that fit him, a bit taller and much slimmer than almost anyone in town. His crisp white shirt billowed in the cool breeze like it was hanging on the wash line. Angelina wore her best black T-shirt, black jeans, and, of course, the green contacts. Juana and Carmen flanked the graveside, watching Father Gilmartin's every move, as if for errors, and scanning the horizon for possible Assembly enemies, until Sheila's coffin was safely in the ground.

"That's your father's house."

Nestor stood outside what was left of a dwelling, slanting to the west on its frame of thick mesquite trunks.

They had driven the twenty miles south from Topowa and through the open gate in a fence that divided O'odham lands into two, indistinguishable tracts of mountainy desert, one in the US and the other in Mexico. More than by any structure, the border was marked by the confluence of two virtual rivers of empty bottles: a stream of clear plastic gallon water jugs discarded by migrants on their way north flowing into the dark brown glass Budweisers left by O'odham partying just south of the line. A few of these locals had already circled there folding chairs and were knocking back beers and burritos supplied by an enterprising Mexican in a taco truck. Among them was Nestor, who then led Angelina and Chico bouncing over another dozen miles of rocky desert trails to *Pozo Verde*.

Chico ducked under the sagging portal of his father's house and into the cool, dark interior, a relief from the sun beating down on his still aching head. His eyes adjusted to find more mesquite uprights, holding the dirt and straw roof aloft. Walls of upright ocotillo sticks, thick and thin, rattled in the wind like a rickety skeleton from which the mud and straw flesh had dried and fallen away. In the very center of the house the walls still held, enclosing in cool darkness traces of the life lived within, a life without Chico and his mother: a cast iron bed with mattress and army blanket nestled in a corner beneath a teddy bear hanging from the wall next to a Guadalupe shrine. The windowsill was covered with rusting tins, arranged before tattered squares of cloth tacked to the collapsing dried window frames where no glass had ever held the outside out.

Chico emerged blinking into the light.

Nestor, putt-putting along in his wheelchair, took them among the other, mostly ruined homes: misshapen adobe blocks melted into orange puddles, ocotillo walls unfurling like fans, the dried mud between the sticks crumbled to dust beneath.

"Did everyone die out of here? Why all the houses are falling down?" Angelina asked.

Nestor backed his chair under what was left of a ramada where they all joined him, finding rocks to sit on.

"No," Nestor replied, "they're mostly just moved out, over the line to Sells or further. Everybody's over there making money, but somehow, they can't come back fix up their houses. They say it's their land, but they don't show it. See, your father was different. I know maybe you don't see it that way 'cause he left you and your mother. But for Pozo Verde it was good that he came back. And he didn't just live here, fix up the old house. He cleared, and he planted. He grew corn and melons, even peach trees there, nearby the spring. He dug the trenches himself for the water to come along. When your father was alive, Pozo Verde was alive. It was O'odham."

"He's there. Along with all the old ones, buried the right way, under stones."

He pointed to the steep and rocky hillside that rose behind the spring.

"Who are the old ones? Do you mean from here, from Pozo Verde?" Angelina asked.

"Them. And others too. Apache spirits."

She turned toward Nestor with the face of a wondering child. Nestor explained.

"Back when the Apache was enemies. More than the Yaqui or the Seri, the Apache was fierce. And when you killed one, there was a lot a power there, and the O'odham used to take the Apache scalp and make a little figure, kinda like a doll. And the O'odham who killed the Apache had to keep that doll with him always. Gave him a lot of power. And when that O'odham died, the Apache doll would be buried along with him. Gave him power beyond and kept the Apache spirit quiet. That's maybe some of the problem we got now."

The word "now" startled his listeners. Wasn't he recounting ancient lore?

"What problem?" Chico asked.

"Everything's all upside down with the People. Gangs. Drugs. More young ones dying than old. That's upside down." He looked pointedly at Angelina.

"What's all that got to do with Apache dolls?" Chico asked.

"Someone is maybe working them dolls. There are families who keep them, which is dangerous enough. Maybe they're doing more with 'em. Up in Sells the earth came scorched."

"You mean all them patches of burnt ground?" Angelina asked, remembering all the talk about mysterious burn marks that appeared in many places in Sells some months earlier. "Didn't they bring all the medicine men and do a big smoke cleansing?"

Nestor leaned forward, staring straight into Angelina's frightened face.

"You think that did anything? If them Apache dolls are making trouble? No, sir. Not if they are still out. All kinds of trouble. Evil. Even to them attacks up in New York."

"9/11?" Angelina blurted out.

Chico almost believed him. In the shadow of that hill with all its gathered O'odham dead and Apache spirits, anything seemed possible.

Including Nestor's very own "chaos theory." Maybe Pozo Verde was the center of more than O'odham land. For her part, Angelina looked more and more like a young O'odham girl. Listening. Hearing.

"Yeah, 9/11. Even old José thinks that. Didn't he walk to *Marena* carrying flags for all them that died? Asked San Francisco for his help, for our people, but for all them too. Violence is our problem. Violence on the Reservation, violence everywhere. So, he walks to *Marena*, José. He's walking now. You two should go there yourself, maybe."

Nestor smiled shyly, and Chico had the feeling of arriving where he had been led: the pilgrimage to *Magdalena—Marena*, the O'odham call it—and the much-revered statue of San Francisco Xavier.

"Go to *Marena*? Now? Right after we bury my mother?"

Nestor leaned forward again and for the first time put his hand on Chico's forearm.

"No. Not after. Before. Take your mother to *Marena*. Maybe you can meet José and the walkers. Take her to see San Francisco," he said, motioning toward the coffin in the back of his pickup. "Then bring her back here."

He nodded toward the hill of graves.

Angelina was looking out the rear cab window, watching the narrow coffin bouncing in the truck bed under its layers of canvas wrapping.

"Are you sure we should be doin' this?"

"Too late to go back, cousin."

Many hours later, they arrived in Tubutama to find that José and the walkers had left two days before and should be nearing the chapel in the tiny desert *ejido* of Cebolla. They followed on the deep blue asphalt road that cut through the open desert until a blinding downpour forced them to find shelter under a trestle that took the road over a wide arroyo.

"There are some pilgrims."

Angelina pointed to a group of sitting figures, huddled together against the dirt bank of the wash.

"Not pilgrims. Migrants."

Though as dark as the O'odham, they were half their size and at their feet were gallon water jugs and backpacks. A woman wearing white sneakers, native serape, and a baseball cap approached the truck. Chico leaned out the window and spoke with her, then translated.

"They're from Chiapas—Indians—and they were told that the local saint could give them a hand, so they are going to Marena before heading for the border."

When the rain slackened, they headed out again, but this time with six *Chiapanecos* in the back of the truck, their piercing black eyes trained on the canvas. Angelina watched through the cab window as the woman—her name was Reina Maria—pulled her serape aside to reveal a baby of about six months huddled against her breast.

"You said they're Indians? Not, like … Mexicans?"

"They are Mexicans—but Indians, from the state of Chiapas. You know, like we're Americans, but Indians from Arizona."

Chico stopped himself from sounding unkind, realizing that Angelina was no different from most O'odham, from most Americans, in seeing no difference among the thousands of nameless migrants struggling across their lands.

"They're Mayans. Got their own language. Some don't even speak Spanish."

"But everybody just calls them *Jujkam*, Mexicans."

Angelina said this not dismissively but with soft confusion. She looked out the little rear window again and saw Reina Maria sliding a hand under the canvas, moving it around until she had touched the wooden coffin, then blessing her child and herself with the same hand.

"What did you tell them we had under the canvas?"

"Our village statue of San Francisco. Why?"

* * *

In the failing light they found the chapel in the ranchito of *Cebolla,* a traditional last stop on the outskirts of Magdalena where pilgrims might sleep before going on to see the Saint in the morning. They arrived just ahead of the walking pilgrims, who had taken a winding dirt path away from the main road. Chico and Angelina found seats on a wooden bench at the front of the tiny chapel. The air inside was heavy with the smell of dry clay and hot with the dozens of candles already lit by a local woman who hoped and believed that San Francisco Xavier would heal her nephew's twisted limb if she prepared and cleaned the chapel every year for the visit of *"mis Indios,"* the O'odham who walked from Tubutama. *Los Chiapanecos*, who were not her *Indios*, were a puzzle. She watched as they slid the canvas-wrapped box from the truck-bed and carried it into the chapel. Could it be that the faithful of San Xavier could now be found so far south as the homeland of these people, who had made the long trek with their village saint? She entered the chapel behind them, blessing herself repeatedly and falling into fervent prayer.

Then the walkers arrived. Chico, Angelina, *los Chiapanecos*, and the local woman turned as one to see the pilgrims enter the chapel, "sung in" by three young men whose broad faces shone with sweat in the candlelight, an O'odham song asking San Francisco to bless their journey. Behind the melody, the rhythmic tapping of staffs on the ancient bricks echoed through the chapel as the pilgrims, softly crying, rounded the altar, touching the statues of the saints and blessing himself, then leaving their staffs—ribboned, feathered, a few painted with stars and stripes—on the altar. There too they left religious pictures and statues, mementos and the personal effects of loved ones living and dead. One woman brought the photograph of the Hopi who was the first US female soldier to die in the Iraq war, another carried the tiny portrait photos—matted together in one large and heavy frame—of every O'odham serving in that other, distant desert. *Los Chiapanecos*, for whom all this was both familiar in spirit and strange in detail, lay the coffin on the brick floor beneath the altar.

The pilgrims filled the benches. Feeling no fatigue, though they had walked for four days, they watched the singers, who stood, still leaning on their staffs, alongside the altar. The lead was a great bear of a man with close-cropped hair and large, square features. His eyes closed, and his tears mingled with his oily sweat as his mind and heart turned inward with the new song he began to sing. The song no one had yet heard. The song the mountain had given him only that morning, turning the thumping course of blood in his aching body into a slow, chanting rhythm. "Oh, San Francisco …."

On the next morning Chico and Angelina brought Sheila into Magdalena to meet the Saint himself, sitting with the coffin in the chapel near the statue while the joyful chaos of his fiesta roared beyond the walls. Parting company with the *Chiapanecos* and the Walkers, they headed back to Pozo Verde.

* * *

Following Nestor's directions, Chico buried Sheila in a sharp crevice in the hillside, marking her grave, like the others, with a heap of stones. Then Nestor handed Chico Sheila's necklace of polished coral and a small stone from the top of the cairn.

"There's always something else to do." Indian wisdom or sardonic commentary?

"Four things. Always four. You took her to Marena. That was good. And you buried her here. Also, good. Now two more things. One journey. Your mother's letter said it."

"About the Ocean?"

"I'itoi's cave looks over the ocean, way out in Pinacate by the sea. That cave is sacred to your aunt Viola's people, the *Hia-Ced* O'odham, who took your mother into their bosom. Time and time on, those people went to the sea to get salt. But they couldn't just take the salt and go back up to their land. The ocean was giving them something of great value, and the ocean was powerful. And dangerous. You don't mess with the ocean. You take away the salt, you leave something behind. Something valuable. So, they would always thank the Ocean and then throw something real important, like a necklace of fine stones, say, into the waves. Now, your mother wasn't going on no salt pilgrimage, but maybe she was down there in Rocky Point one time and left without giving, and so the Ocean come after her. Maybe cause she left the 'Hia-Ced Way' all the gods were after her, with all that Assembly shit she was doing."

Chico could see where Nestor was going with this, and Angelina was already smiling and shaking her head.

"You gotta go to the Ocean. Maybe your mother's spirit is gonna roam restless, you see? Maybe go wandering for the ocean. Maybe disturbing others. You gotta go there right away, follow the Hia-Ced path through the Pinacate, to I'itoi's cave, then through the dunes to the sea."

Nestor continued, now looking at Angelina.

"You will go with Chico to I'itoi's cave. Help him."

Angelina reached over and touched Chico's arm. Little and Big Sister.

Then to Chico, "Leave the stone from your mother's grave with I'itoi. Then go to the ocean. You ask a pardon for your mother and throw her necklace into the waves. That's one thing you gotta do for sure. And San Francisco's gonna go with you now."

Somehow, Chico had no difficulty with the notion that he needed throw a silver-plated chain of coral with a tiny cross into the sea, or that a Jesuit saint would help him in this mission to placate the O'odham spirits, angry with his Irish mother. And so, before dawn the next day, Nestor drove them one hundred miles west across the desert to the edge of the Pinacate, the great volcanic wilderness through which they had to walk, up the increasingly rugged, basalt black hills, the greater heights seeming only to bring them closer to the punishing sun.

He wakes from the turtle dream, his neck aching and his shirt sticking to his back with sweat. Rising too quickly, dizzy in the sun, he is suddenly doubled over with cramping pain in the gut, falling to his knees, his hands gripping the rocky earth. And vomiting. Heaving dry and empty, over, and over again. Angelina leans over him and with a hand laid gently on his back, soothes and cossets his shaking body. He draws slow, deep breaths, and rises.

They are walking again, and the quaking emptiness becomes a lightness of step and of mind. It is midday now and they must cover many miles to reach the pointed peak that shimmers white above the desert before them. The land appears as broad stripes of color: black, cream white, light green, then darker green rising over hummocky rocks. Above that tower the gray-white granite walls and peaks of the great, silent volcano. The black is a lava flow, a wall that rises twenty feet above the cindered ground of the desert floor and then continues, an undulating table of great and small pieces of volcanic spew. The ragged, evil-looking fragments are lost in their own black shadows beneath the afternoon sun, but for the topmost pieces that stand, edges tilted up, like frantic spirits against the sky. There is a good path to the peak that leads in a great loop around this angry field. But crossing through it, though difficult, would take miles and hours off their journey.

Chico weighs the choice, but Angelina has already moved ahead of him up onto the edge of the lava flow, picking her way along it with unexpected delicacy and grace. Suddenly, she stops in her tracks: a still, brown body on the black rocks. Chico follows her eyes along the broken black ridges to the dark silhouette of a ram among the sinister rocks. Leaving the shielding shadow of a higher lava shelf, the ram moves closer and Chico sees his quizzing eyes and wonderful horns, curving out and back, then under, so that the points come forward again. Two smaller, female, heads pop up from among the rocks behind. Then all three step away, light and sure as if they are on flat and easy ground, appearing and disappearing in the rise and fall of the lava flow, moving steadily west toward the peak.

The cousins follow. Rocks, light with pockets of gas, shift, crunch and ring hollow beneath their feet as they clatter and spring off them: ankles firm, thighs pumping a rhythm propelling them forward. As if they were on the surface of water into which they would sink if ever they stopped. And when any rock, as solid-seeming as the earth itself, teeters like a seesaw beneath their feet, they turn the fall forward, mountain-sheep-like, landing a stiff hoof on the next rock. Finally, they leave the lava for the *playa*, hard-packed sand studded with greasewood, where they move quickly, their thirst a hard-edged lump in the back of the throat, until they reach the base of *Sierra Suvuk*, a line of low granite mountains like ships reefed on the sands.

This was the site of summer fields for Aunt Viola's people, the Hia-Ced O'odham.

We dam up where the wash comes around by Suvuk.

Viola had so well described the place that Chico recognizes the wide *arroyo*, a river of sand that speaks of waters rushing over it, bringing life to scattered trees and thick shrubs hugging its edges. They find shade under one of them, a hardy ironwood whose roots buckle over the rocks and foliage, sinking into the soft sands to drink up whatever moisture lies beneath.

He can hear again Viola's instructive voice.

Up there where it comes around from above the black rocks. We dam it there and then the rains come and slide out over the thirsty ground around the wash. And then our seeds come up. Pumpkins, squash, beans, even watermelon. One big rain and they are growing good.

It is many years since crops were grown here, but even though there has not been rain in this part of the desert for several months, the mesquite leaves are deep green.

The animals will tell you where it is. Viola again.

Tracks lead everywhere in the wash, crisscrossing cats, birds of every size, tail-dragging kangaroo rats, tiny-footed desert chipmunks. Then his eye catches the fresher sign of a coyote, crossing atop the others and making his sure way up the *arroyo*. Chico's own clan after all, Coyote, something he hasn't thought much about for many years.

"This way," he says to Angelina and he follows the spoor dropped that very morning and cuts the sign again where the paws scraped over the rocks at the base of Suvuk. He feels the coyote's thirst as his own, and quickens his pace between granite boulders, shimmying up to a clear shelf where a small natural tank hides under a dark, overhanging rock. Water.

* * *

The climb to I'itoi's cave is not difficult and, renewed with the water, they arrive just as the shadows disappear and the rocks gray into one another. In the dark, the heat of the desert vanishes upward as if the gods have opened the sky like a lid. Chico unfurls the sleeping bags next to one another and looks about in the last visible moments for a few sticks to make a fire. But there are none this high and they settle in side by side, looking up into the brilliant bands of stars. From there, high as they are, there are no earthly lights to be seen.

They have said very little to one another all day, so Angelina's voice, low and soft though it is, startles Chico.

"Do you think this will work? I mean, will this help your mother? Will it help you?"

Chico looks over, unsure of her expression in the dark, and laughs softly.

"I don't know if anything works—or if anything much can help me … or my mother."

He sighs and then continues.

"Sometimes I think that the last time anything made sense to me was back in my Crips and Bloods days. I knew who I was then. We all did. You could feel it every time you tied on your colors. When you walked with your boys. Sometimes you could even feel your own blood was flowing with theirs—like in one beat. You lost yourself—whatever bullshit things you had going—and then found yourself again, only bigger."

Chico can see Angelina's green eyes now, sparkling in the night like the stars.

"Funny, but the army didn't seem that different at first. Beat the shit out of you until you loved them. They always talk about how they make a man of you, like you were gonna be real macho, real hard—like no feeling. But, it's the opposite. It's all about love. That's how they get you to fight and die, not because of fear, or courage. Because of love. Love the country. Love the flag. Love duty. Love your army brothers. But each love gets less real the longer you slog through a desert so far from home. In the end, only your brothers are real. Make sense. And you stop thinking so much about any of the rest."

Angelina isn't sure how what he means but is thrilled by the intimacy of his words.

Suddenly he is smiling and reaching over to put his hand on her shoulder.

"But here I am in another desert, in some other kinda pain, trying to remember what I forgot, or maybe what I never knew … and, maybe it will feel different tomorrow, but tonight I feel like it *will* work, like it *does* makes sense, like I know where I—where we—are going."

In the morning they awake stiff and cold. They have slept right at the entrance of the cave, a wide hole wind-worn in the rock that doesn't seem big enough to have sheltered their ancestors, as the stories tell, from the Spanish. Or to house a god. But when they go inside to place the stone from Sheila's cairn on I'itoi's rough altar, Chico feels the cool chamber open like the night sky, making its own infinity. Angelina's eyes are moist as she touches the wall of the cave, letting her fingers trail lightly along its surface, like a blind woman reading Braille.

* * *

"There it is! The sea!"

Angelina is up above Chico. She has managed to crawl out on a rock shelf and, leaning hard against the mountain, has carefully rounded the cliff to where she can see to the west. The volcanic world, so vast and encompassing, drops off just there, what seems like only a mile or two away, where the mountains meet waves, not yet of water, but of sand: a sea of perfect rolling white dunes that stretch for some few miles again to the west. But over the crests of the farthest row she sees a deep green stripe beneath the cobalt sky. The ocean.

The dunes are in fact close. But the water is farther than it seems. The sands, like the water, always play with the pilgrim, each dune coming close, but withdrawing as he goes forward. Each crest attained only reveals more on the horizon. Always more. And walking on sand proves more difficult than on angry rocks; ground that yields does not push you forward.

At last they reach the last high line of dunes, and from there the sand falls gently, sloping to a broad beach. Though the shanks of her legs are stiffened and aching, Angelina runs to the edge of the water, where the white foam surf curls into the gravelly sand. The waves are not high, but the meeting place of sea and earth is very long, stretching beyond sight to the north and south. The sound is strong, a grinding roar that befits a great border.

Chico stands for a moment beside her at the water's edge and then, shedding most of his clothing, takes a running dive through the breaking wave. He strokes quickly out beyond the shallows, where the cooler current caresses and awakens his skin as he dives deep into the clear waters, brightened by the sun's rays that reach down to illuminate a world busy with shape and movement. And color. Soft purple seaweed undulates over stones encrusted with bright green or red coral, and schools of yellow, metallic blue, and black fish the size of large coins flicker about as if to music.

He opens his hand and watches his mother's necklace drop down through the watery forest, the cross seeming to scatter the tiny fish.

And then, submitting to another impulse, he pulls a thin chain off over his head and lets it go as well, watching the slower swirl of its lighter metal and the glittering silver flash of the dog tags finding the sea floor.

7

Ranch Rescue

Fig. 7.1 Photograph by Maeve Hickey

Gil Orozco takes aim for the third time and squeezes the trigger, trying to ignore the snickering boys. But this time the metal disk pings sharply and *Los Tigres del Norte* marionettes jangle to life, jolting about on their strings, flailing little guitars to the loud, tinny strains of the *narcotraficante corrido*. A cheer goes up—the boys are as pleased with his success as they have been with his failure.

He smiles, puts down the rifle, and wanders off past the carnival rides toward the square. The fiesta is in full swing, fueled by a prodigious flow of *Tecate* beer and lit by looping strings of naked bulbs, hanging from power lines, and hissing flames leaping up from dozens of rolling food carts. Sinaloa brass bands face off across the streets, trumpets blaring while drunken *vaqueros* sway and dip, alone or with partners, unfazed by the competing cacophonies. Most charmed by this theater are the poorest pilgrims, those who have come farthest and from the smallest places to see San Francisco.

Yes, the Saint is there. Beyond the hawkers and the rows of *puestos* selling sweets, trinkets, and cures. Beyond the shops selling statues of Our Lady, San Judas, San Martín, and hundreds of black-robed plastic San Franciscos in their see-through caskets. Beyond all that, the Saint "himself" lies within the chapel at the side of *La Iglesia Misión de Magdelena de Kino*, receiving the faithful. They have come to fulfill their promises, their *mandas*, and now file, weary but deeply happy, past the reclining figure, regarding him with humble adoration, caressing his wooden feet, his knees, his head. They leave coins in the box, and their photos, hair braids, letters, even sonograms and hospital wristbands, on the chapel windowsills.

Gil falls in behind a group of pilgrims who, like himself, are shorter and darker than most. They are also more tentative, and yet more focused with desperate intent than the other pilgrims. One of them is a young woman who, when she reaches the Saint, seems transformed by hope, running a hand with great tenderness and affection over the wooden body, and then lifting her toddler to kiss San Francisco's already lipstick-stained face.

Reina Maria, who has followed the other migrants to the safe house, holds Pacito and watches through the only window, a square of dirty glass roughly set in the brick wall. Across the road, a slight, gentle-seeming young man stands under a naked streetlight and checks the address on the scrap of paper a third time. Satisfied that he is in the right place, he walks too quickly across the night street, stumbling in a shallow pothole on the way, and is admitted to the house. Reina Maria thinks she may have seen him the day before in the chapel with San Francisco. He tells the boy his name, Gilberto, and is about to escape into the shadows with the others, when the door swings open again and in steps the *coyote*: short, big-gutted, ugly as a toad.

He takes Gil's money and smoothly folds the bills into his wallet, running a deliberate, cold eye over the new *pollo*, from his shoes right up to his face. Gil tries not to squirm. Does the *coyote* sense that he is not comfortable in his clothes, that though he has the dark face of the others, he hasn't their expression?

The *coyote* crunches a *chicharone* slowly between his teeth and then, smiling broadly, turns to address the migrants.

"*Que se pongan cómodos, pasan la noche aquí.*"

No one asks why they aren't crossing that night, or when they would be crossing, or what would happen next. Blankets are silently unfurled. Men light cigarettes, and women settle their children. Gil unrolls the tattered sleeping bag he'd found in a thrift shop a few days earlier, and, propping his backpack under his head, stares at the long cracks in the ceiling until they disappear in the gloom, breathing in air redolent of home-made corn tortillas and cheap tobacco.

He wonders for the hundredth time what he is doing and hears once again the voice of his sister.

"You believe you can relive all that by taking a bus? A ride in a truck? Even a long walk? That's like thinking you are a Catholic if you sit through one Mass. It is your trip you are taking, not anybody else's. Not hers."

Her light skin makes her haughty, he thinks, trying to distract himself from any sting of truth. "His trip." What did she know of that? She can't imagine what it has always been like for him. After all, she looks like their father. He, on the other hand, is the *moreñito*, the little dark one, whose Indian features never fail to surprise him in the morning mirror. And she seems so comfortable in both languages, even though their parents have spoken only English to them. It had been enough for her to hear them with one another, and to pick up every sly intonation on the street. She moves effortlessly through that American world, as comfortable in her fluent Arizona Spanglish as she is in her changing Chicana fashions.

For him, nothing has fit easily. Shame made him turn away from the language as a boy, only to send him reeling back to it years later, when he took his first trip with his mother to the village of her birth.

"*Con el nopal en la frente!* With the prickly pear in his face! Yet he doesn't speak the language."

That's what they said, laughing at the incongruity, but also hurt at what they saw as a repudiation. So, he set out to make up lost ground, straining to remember the voices of his childhood behind the barking conjugations of an Argentinean high school teacher. But his compulsion could take him only so far. He sought an already perfect idiom that he could don like a magic cloak, rendering him invisible beneath, rather than a lover with whom he might grow and learn to hear and speak the world anew.

There is a rustle of bedclothes just beyond his ear, and Gil half-turns to see a baby boy's face blinking in the deepening shadows, brown crumbs clinging to his lips. The small voice of its young mother comes floating from the darkness behind.

"*Quieres un taco?*"

A hand passes over the child's shoulder with her offering.

"*Muchas gracias.*"

He bites through the comforting warm corn tortilla and into the spicy paste of beans and chiles around which it is rolled, wishing he had a dozen more and some rich, sweet black coffee to wash them down.

Her voice comes again, and now he can nearly make out her slim form, sitting cross-legged beyond her child.

"*De donde eres?*"

Where am I from? He pauses for a moment before answering.

"*Rancho de la Ciénega, en el sur de Puebla.*"

He tries to speak in the accent of his mother. It sounds wrong to him, as if he were somehow exaggerating, but his doubts are only his own and his new friend is at her ease with a young man she imagines shares her world as well as her language.

"*Soy Gilberto. Y tú?*"

"*Reina María. Tienes familia por otro lado?*"

She hands him another rolled tortilla as she speaks.

"*Si, en Arizona—no tan lejos de la línea.*"

"*Qué suerte! Soy de Chiapas, de San Ramón. Un pueblito.* Only a couple of hundred of us left there. All old men, women and children. All the others are on the other side. My husband and three brothers too."

She thrusts a small scrap of paper into his hand. He reads the crooked, looping letters: "Nebraska." Beneath it is a phone number.

"I have to make my way with this one"—she says, nodding toward the child—"all the way there. Do you know the place? I am told it is very far from the border."

She talks on like this for a while, describing her home, the way it was before so many left and the way it is now; how her brothers have gone, one after the other, to that place on the paper; how her new husband—who has not yet seen his son—finally forsook the uncharitable fields of his homeland, sending back money to his parents as well as to her, for their passage. She has traveled by bus with this little band of fellow villagers, crossing the mountains and fields, arriving in the scorching desert town of Altar. They had decided to come to Magdalena first before heading for the border, having heard about the power of San Francisco. Like Gilberto, they had been approached in the square and handed a piece of paper with this address.

She speaks in the soft singsong of her region, a nearly unbroken river of words, punctuated only by an occasional pause when she hands Gilberto another taco, rolled while she speaks, over the now sleeping child. Nothing she says goes beyond the sort of things that strangers might speak of on a bus, but her words take on a mysterious and intimate beauty, rising and falling disembodied through this night chamber full of strangers, all of them slipping into sleep in a dark before a dawn when anything might happen.

But they are up and out before the first light, herded into the back of large pickup, and then rolling at high speed northward to Imuris and then east to the border town of *Agua Prieta*, which faces across the border to Douglas, Arizona, and the rough grass hills of the expansive desert ranches that abound in that region. They file silently out of the truck at the edge of the *plazuela*, finding shaded benches or patches of cool grass beneath trees where they are to wait for another nightfall.

Gilberto has disliked border towns all his life, believing that Nogales—where his father's family still lived—could not be Mexico, but rather a deeply tainted bastard child. Now, however, he sits confused on his bench in a little plaza in another border town, Agua Prieta, surrounded by the performing presence of the entire country. All Mexico is here, and on the move. It seems as if every other private home has been converted into a guesthouse, *una casa de huespedes*, for the hundreds of would-be migrants arriving daily. Shop windows are full of water jugs, backpacks, flashlights, and the combination nail-clipper can-openers favored now for the journey, some plain, but most decorated with an American flag and the Virgin of Guadalupe.

Across the square beyond the two great spreading umbrella trees, he can make out an American family: the husband in a straw hat and the wife in a sun visor, both wear blindingly white sneakers. Behind them troop a sullen young teenaged girl and her annoying ten-year-old brother. Already burdened with several great clay pots and some feathered sticks of uncertain provenance or purpose, they are still in a buying mood, and every vendor they amble by is trying his best American English sales banter on them.

"Don't cross the street! I got the same junk over here!"

Above the family, three US soldiers are relaxing on the shaded balcony of *El Oasis*, sucking on the morning-after, lime-stuffed necks of bottles of Corona, and checking out the passing Mexican women, who move through an altogether different space. They are bringing children to school, going off to work at the *maquiladoras*, the assembly plants on the edge of town, or coming to relax for a few moments, like Gilberto, on a bench beneath the heavily leafed, bird-chattering trees, where they speak with a friend or watch their neighbors enter and emerge from the busy parish church on the edge of the square.

The American mother shouts, calling her family together to begin the short walk back to the borderline. They will cross unquestioned and unquestioning, walking a few hundred yards to their car parked safely in the US. They had come to that side just as easily, simply entering through the gate into "Mexico-Land" and walking about it like they would any other vacation theme park in their own country. They seem not to notice the guesthouses or the dozens of other visitors to the town arrayed around the square, backpacks at their sides. Gilberto tries for a moment to despise them but is struck rather by their fleshy normality.

Hours later, dizzy from wandering the streets, he is back at the *plazuela* and sees some of the others again, silently huddled on benches to be close to one another. He makes his way over to them, sensing that the unmoving form lying on a bench, wrapped in a blanket under the shade of a cottonwood, is Reina Maria and her child. Her black hair emerges from the serape and shimmers in the light, and then her face suddenly appears, eyes clouded by sleep, but hands already moving deftly to pull her child out into the sunlight.

"*Hola*," he says quietly and finds the place made for him next to her.

She smiles sweetly and now for the first time he sees that she is beautiful—sharp-featured with wide Mayan eyes—but young, no more than nineteen or twenty. Without a word she puts the child in his lap while she recovers from her siesta, straightening her hair and clothes. Seeing that the child is happy enough with Gilberto, she leaves him there and leans over toward the next bench to talk with another young woman. When the sun begins to set, they all rise together, Gilberto feeling as if he were moving in a dream until he lifts little Pacito and feels his warm weight against his chest and shoulder.

As dawn breaks, they find themselves several miles inside the US.

So far, the trip has been uneventful. Gilberto squeezed in the back with the others. Reina Maria was somewhere across the truck bed with her fellow *Chiapanecos*. He could see little but felt the journey over the changing surfaces of the road: cobblestones, crumbling tarmac, washboard dirt and then the surprisingly smoother ride across the packed desert sand when Gilberto managed to poke his head out from between the two thick men wedged in against him and over the side of the pickup. He felt like a child in the back of his father's truck, a soft breeze in his face, admiring how the driver threaded his way between widely spaced clumps of desert plants. When they reached the border fence, which looked no more important than any ranch boundary, a boy leaped from the cab and, grasping an upright fence pole tightly in his two hands, simply lifted it out of ground and opened the eight-foot section of barbed wire like a gate. The truck rumbled through, and the fence was closed behind them.

Now the first rays of gray light show a landscape no different from that on the other side of the fence. The same *saguaro* shadows fall across hard, yellow earth studded with bunch grass and gray fists of creosote. There is still no sign of Border Patrol anywhere around, just as their *coyote* had promised. No sign of anybody or anything to say that they are in a different country.

The truck stops abruptly at the edge of sandy trail. The *coyote* jumps out and strolls over to a small hillock from which he surveys the surrounding country while smoking a cigarette. When he finishes, he walks casually back to the truck, opens the tailgate, and tells the group to descend.

"*Todos tienen su agua?*" he says to them, holding up a gallon plastic jug like a flight attendant preparing passengers for a safe voyage. "Follow this path north, but stay well off it, there in the scrub. *La Migra* will see any tracks you leave in the path. You will go no more than three or four miles and then you will come to a large *arroyo*. There you will be met by another truck. Wait for it. They will take you the rest of the way."

There is no explanation offered for this change of plan. Nothing about why the *coyote* will not take them all the way to their destination. A couple of them fidget nervously, but while Gil stands dumbstruck, watching as the truck turns around and bounces over the desert back toward the border, the others are already trudging off through the yielding sand.

Several hours later, he realizes that they have gone more than three or four miles, more like six he thinks, and there has been no sign of any wash. He has been walking alongside Reina Maria, who has been slowed by the weight of her restless Pacito. They have not seen the others for some time, and now they face a choice; the path branches off in two directions, northeast and northwest.

"Look," Reina Maria says, pointing to the easily visible tracks the others have left a few yards to the right of the path leading to the northeast.

La Migra will have no difficulty following them, Gil thinks, feeling a brief temptation to go the way of the footprints, to add the experience of arrest to this re-enactment, but points instead in the other direction.

"Let's go this way but keep well away from the path."

An hour's walk brings them into rougher terrain, where a rocky outcrop offers the possibility of shaded rest through the worst part of the afternoon. Then they continue northwest in the declining light, walking until the full dark reveals the shimmering blanket of stars above them. Though tired, they move more quickly in the cooling night, now with lighter water jugs and taking turns with Pacito, who breathes more easily in the night air. But they will need to stop soon, Gilberto knows, to rest and make a fire for the child's sake, even though they will risk being discovered.

They keep the fire small and low, scraps of mesquite and the strange latticework of cactus skeletons burning in a hole protected by a ring of rocks. The fire, Gilberto reasons, cannot be seen, and the smoke will be nearly invisible in the night. They nestle in beside it, Reina Maria's serape stretching across the three figures dwarfed in the night desert.

Though she is glad to be with Gilberto, his presence makes her even lonelier. It has been more than a year since she last saw her husband, and his features refuse to take certain shape before her closed eyes. She opens them only to find Gilberto's vulnerable, delicate face, looking distant and sad. He must be missing someone as well.

"Tell me about your village in Puebla."

"It was my mother's village."

He thinks of his mother, of her story of *el rancho*, so vivid and heard so early and often in his childhood that it merged with the memories of places he had himself been. For years, he nearly believed that he had been born there, or at least brought in mewling infancy to bathe in the brown water of the small stream, and cough in the smoke of the village barbecue on the feast day, when his uncles trooped through the tiny hillside hamlet with their precious *Virgencita* on a palette. It was a fantasy he might have held on to if only he had not been taken there and walked the shabby paths and met the friendly but somehow distant faces of its—of his mother's—people. The conjured rancho vanished, taking even his imagined memories with it.

"I went there when I was a young teenager. Painful. I never returned until last week, this time to face the cousins and all the others, only to find that they had left, just like in your place. All of them gone to El Norte. The village was more than sad; it was broken, defeated."

Reina Maria listens carefully, imagining that he, like herself, had been brought up by his mother on stories of her own village, of the always better place that young women must leave when they marry. And that the village in which he had himself been raised was farther along the same valley, or just over the mountain wall that always divides one little kingdom from the next in that part of the world.

"Was your own place nearby? Or far from there?"

"Very far."

He has reached the point of no return.

"I grew up—I was born—in Tucson. My father is Sonoran, from Nogales. My mother met him in Nogales when she crossed. Then they moved to Tucson, where my father learned to fix cars."

She thinks she must have misheard him.

"I don't understand. You are American?"

"Yes."

"You have papers and everything?"

Reina Maria rises, taking her son with her, as if ready to carry him out of the way of the danger she now senses.

"Why did you lie? Why are you crossing like this?"

She is not loud, but her tone is shrill, her eyes great and hollow with confused anger. Although she cannot see the relevance of his lie to her own journey, she is afraid that she has been tricked for the second time, and to be tricked is her greatest fear. All the migrants speak of it. At best, she would lose her money. At worst … there were too many worsts.

He reaches for Reina Maria's hand, but she withdraws it quickly.

"You told me last night of your journey here, of your fears and hopes. I have heard that same story from my own mother. I needed to see what it was like for myself, to live that story, maybe to write about it."

"You are going to write what I told you? What we said last night? You will take away my name, my story, and put it in a book?"

Can she possibly like the idea? For a moment, she seems happy. But she is only excited at her own understanding, that she has grasped what was up until then unfathomable. She has put a name on a formless treachery.

"*Chingate!* Fuck you!"

She nearly whispers this and spins around, walking away a few paces.

A coyote howls beyond the hills, reminding Gilberto of where they are. Their water is nearly finished, and the child will not last long in the desert.

"Look."

He speaks quietly, following her to the edge of the light thrown by their small fire.

"I won't write anything about you. In fact, I won't write anything at all. I had thought that I would be able to relive or to find something…"

"That you are missing?"

She finishes his sentence, speaking more softly already, though she is still angry.

"Did your mother leave you, or die? It is only a motherless child who searches like that. Or was it only that she pushed you away from the breast too soon?"

He thinks of saying that it has more to do with finding out who he is, with the confusions of race and language. Of crossing a border that is inscribed on his very soul. She cannot know about that, could not imagine it, and so sees things in the starker, simpler terms in which she speaks. Of mothers and children. It is Pacito who breaks the silence, crying in hunger. Reina Maria lifts him and takes out a small, golden breast swollen with milk, the deep brown nipple hard and round for the hungry child in her arms. Gilberto turns painfully away and goes back to the fire, settling himself in the sleeping bag and staring up at the incredible sky, watching meteorites unseen in Tucson chase across the galaxies.

Sometime in the middle of the night he feels her come near, stooping, opening his sleeping bag and crawling in next to him, taking Pacito with her. The three of them breathe as one, heavily but sweetly, and fall as one into dreaming sleep. Pacito dreams of the sheltering warmth about him, Reina Maria of a husband's floating, unsettled face, and Gilberto of Reina Maria's golden breasts. He feels them, so he dreams, pressed against his back, circles of warm silk, the nipples hardening again into pebbles. He turns and puts a hand over each breast, lightly brushing them with his palms, and then brings one hand up to the downy hair on the back of her neck and lets it slide slowly down following the curve of her spine, coming to rest on the small, taut globes beneath. Squeezing, he pulls her gently but firmly toward himself, till every part of her touches every part of him, and her lips find his in the dark. They kiss deeply while Pacito's breathing falls into a yet heavier, comforting drone behind them. And while they continue to kiss, she takes him in her warm hand, slow and confident, playing her fingers on the surface till all thought is gone and his only feeling is there, pulsing, as her hand now tightens around him and guides him into her, inner fingers seeming to work as the outer ones did, softly insistent, pulling and kneading. He isn't sure whether he is still dreaming, but their hips move together, firmly, urgently, until, his nails digging into her and hers into him, they erupt into a common shudder, then slowly melt into one another and find a dreamless sleep.

They make love once again just before dawn breaks, this time fully awake, seeing one another's dark faces in the first gray light, kissing less greedily but with slow softness. He raises himself on his arms to watch her breasts move like waves beneath him.

Pacito is awake and bringing Reina Maria back from another deep sleep when she hears the jeep, its diesel strokes getting louder by the second.

"Gilberto!"

He nearly leaps from the sleeping bag, but it is already too late. The jeep mounts the last rise and descends on them like a judgment. The driver, a heavy man, thin lips stretched tight in grim determination, wears a large white western hat and sunglasses. Next to him is a tall red-haired man in a plaid shirt and baseball cap, grinning demonically. He cradles the rifle in his lap like a favorite child. The jeep comes to a stop in a cloud of dust and the men approach, the tall one pointing his rifle at them, still grinning.

"Well, fuck me, if we don't have a tribe of them here, no papers I'm guessing, and trespassing on private property. Mine to be exact. And there are no papers that allow that. Isn't that right, Jake?"

The driver only laughs.

Reina Maria looks at Gil in confusion and terror. She understands nothing of what they say. The jeep is unmarked. No lights or sirens, and the men are not wearing uniforms. She has seen enough in Mexico to know that men who point guns and laugh are doubly dangerous. The red-haired man with the gun speaks again.

"Okay, folks, we are taking you in. Citizen's arrest."

He walks over to Reina Maria, and nudging her with the end of the rifle, says, "Why don't we just do her here, huh?"

The driver laughs again.

"And get sand in my pants? I don't think so."

More laughter.

Reina Maria is still looking helplessly at Gil.

"Tell them you are American. Show them your papers and tell them we were just married, and my papers are coming!"

"*Americano*? What's that about *Americano*?"

It is the driver; he removes his cowboy hat to wipe his brow and frowns. The other man points the rifle more emphatically.

"Get in the fucking jeep."

They climb in the back and Gil whispers quickly to Reina Maria.

"They aren't *Migra*. They are ranchers, and more dangerous. Let me think what to do, what to say."

Pacito begins to cry softly.

The ride to the ranch is short. About a mile to the north they meet a dirt road; another two miles and they are there. The rifle still at their back, they stoop to enter a large chicken coop where the others they had walked with are already waiting. They nearly smile to see one another.

One of the others explains that they too had walked without finding the fabled wash but had in the night finally come out onto the road, and while they stood deciding what to do, along came the jeep. Then a truck arrived and took them all to the ranch.

"We were afraid you had died in the desert," the poor captive continued. "We shouldn't have let you fall behind. But it is all the fault of that *pinché coyote, verdad?*"

Gil still says nothing, deciding it is better to listen first to the loud conversation just outside the bunkhouse.

"Did you call the Patrol yet?"

It is the voice of the fat man, the driver of the jeep.

"Yeah, Jake, I called them." Now the red-haired man with the gun is speaking.

"They're in no hurry. Said as long as we've got 'em safe here, they'll be by with the van at the end of the shift. So, looks like they're spending the day here."

"This is turning into something a lot more complicated than I pictured."

It was another voice, perhaps an older one.

"I mean this started as us just making sure the Border Patrol did their job on our lands here. You told me that we were gonna call them in when we spotted illegals. But Christ, those bastards never manage to get here in time to do anything, so we end up doing their job for them. Well, I don't fucking like it. Thank God none of 'em ever runs, cause Pete over there would probably shoot one."

"Fucking right I would." (It is the voice of the red-haired man.)

"Yeah, well maybe you would, but I wouldn't. I don't want these people crossing my land. I don't want them in the US without papers. And I will even go as far as holdin' them till the Patrol gets their fannies over here. But I don't think they need shootin', and I sure as fuck don't want to be the one shootin' them."

"Well, nobody's shootin' anybody, Henry."

"No, not yet anyway. But I am telling you I don't like this arrangement we've gotten ourselves into here. Holding a dozen people. These here aren't in too bad a shape, but sometimes they are, and one could die on us that way. And now we've got that girl and her baby, couldn't be more than a few months old. Now what if something happens with that kid? You want to be a party to that, Jake?"

"Fuck, Henry. Don't you think that baby had a much better chance of dying in the desert than here, with food, water, and shade?"

"I suppose, but we have sure gone way past spotting and calling. We are fucking mixed up in their lives."

They walk away. Gilberto tries to think about what he should do and how he can do it. There is no question of leading an insurrection but finding a way to get himself and the girl and Pacito out. Maybe he can use what she said, about being American, about being married. He needs a way to talk to Henry, the one who doesn't like what they are doing.

"Hey!" Gil calls out the window, in English, but with the lilt and accent of a border ranchhand. "I need to talk to Henry."

Pete, the red-haired man with the gun, on whose ranch they are imprisoned, answers.

"Who the hell said that? How do you know Henry?"

"Man, I worked for him. He knows me! Tell him I'm Gilberto, Pedro's cousin."

"Wait a fucking minute."

He hears the boots crunching off and then returning with another man. Pete opens the door to the chicken coop, still holding his rifle, and motions Gilberto, who is the only one standing, outside.

"You say you worked for me?" Henry asks. He is a large man, something above sixty years old, looking and sounding unsure, and that is the most Gilberto has hoped for.

"Yeah. It was a long time ago. But I am American, with a passport and everything. Born in Tucson, then back to my family's place in Mexico, then back here. You know the way, back and forth."

Gil smiles ingratiatingly and fishes in his pants leg, bringing up the passport.

"It looks real, all right. But if you are a citizen, what the fuck are you doing out there with the others?"

"It's the girl and the baby. They are mine. It happened when I was visiting family down there. Now she wants to come up and join me here. I love her, but we are not yet married, and she has no papers. I told her I will go down and cross her, then we get married up here and apply for papers, everything. And we would have made it too if that fucking cheat of a Mexican *coyote* hadn't left us in the middle of nowhere. I didn't know what to do, because that guy with the gun, he's crazy. Then I heard your voice and hoped you would remember me, even though it is a long time ago. I was a kid, maybe sixteen, and I only worked for a few weeks, helping my cousin Pedro with the roundup."

That was plausible, Henry thought. He had nearly forty years of roundups under his belt, with God knows how many "Pedros" and their cousins showing up on their way through to somewhere else. Mostly illegals too, and he had a moment of trouble over the inconsistency of his position, hiring some, arresting others.

Henry is saying nothing, just looking uncomfortable and no doubt considering his options. "I know you will let me go," Gil says, pushing it a bit, but smiling softly all the while. Because, after all, you cannot hold an American citizen like this. But I am hoping you will do me the great kindness of letting the girl and child go with me. I am truthful with you, man-to-man. She has no papers. You can hold her and the baby. But they are my family now and I ask you man-to-man for your help."

Gil isn't smiling now, but instead looks deep and unflinchingly into Henry's eyes, as he would expect an American equal to do.

"Alright. Go back inside now, till I figure something out."

Henry says this before he can really think through what he is promising. The others will not like it one bit. Pete might even want to hold on to Gil and let the Patrol decide if his passport is genuine. Gil waits back inside, holding on to Reina Maria and Pacito, afraid to say anything yet. An hour passes before Henry opens the door and motions for him to come out.

He speaks quickly and quietly.

"I'm gonna let you go now, but we won't say anything to anybody about the girl and baby. You tell her to keep her mouth shut. Get yourself down this road here to the fork, it's only about two miles. Go down the *arroyo* cutting off to the left, and in about a mile or so you'll come to a waterhole with a small cabin next to it. You wait in there. Tonight, just after dark, the girl should start yelling that her baby's sick, that he's got a fever. I'll come in and get her and the kid and say I'm taking them off to a doctor down my way. I'll drop her off where you're at. Guess I'll say that she jumped out and ran off."

Gil can't believe his luck. He thanks Henry and re-enters the chicken coop, whispering the plan to Reina Maria, then adding, "Tell the others that I had worked for the kind one and that he let me go. Say nothing more. I'll see you this evening."

He picks up his sack, kisses Reina Maria, tousles Pacito's hair, and calls through the window for Henry, who opens the door and lets him out.

An hour later Gil has found the shack and made himself comfortable inside it, escaping the afternoon heat that is already blistering the world outside. He lies on a wooden bench, the only piece of furniture in the place, in the darkest corner of the shack, watching a black wolf spider edge along the wall, looking for dinner. He sips the water Henry had given him as he left the ranch and for the first time feels his hunger. A rummage through his rucksack turns up the last stick of beef jerky. He proceeds to slowly devour half of it, ripping off small pieces with his teeth, chewing each one vigorously for a minute and then letting it sit in his mouth, the smoky, salty juices dripping down and stinging the back of his throat.

There is a noise outside. It could of course be anything, but, somehow, he is sure it is human: a tentative halting, a changing step, a faltering footfall. He sits upright, listening, and then goes out into the late afternoon sun, picking his way through a small stand of short but sprawling mesquites, to find himself at the edge of the waterhole Henry had spoken of. On the other side, no more than thirty feet away, two spotted cows crouch in the shade watching the flies dance over the water. But it was not their movements he had heard. The white forms scattered over the ground just beyond the cows are gallon water jugs. Empties. Like those he'd seen scattered through the desert during his ride with his uncle. Gil smiles. He is far from the first migrant to pass this way, though probably the only one to be invited to wait in the stark comfort of the cabin. The others would have moved furtively through the mesquite bosque, drawing the precious water from the hole, all the time eyeing the cabin with longing and suspicion, listening for any sound, and, if they heard one, scattering into dry grass and stumpy yucca beyond. That, Gil realizes with chagrin, was the noise he heard. The fearful retreat of migrants who sensed what they took to be a menacing presence in the cabin.

"*Dios Mio! Mi bebé está enfermo! Por favor! Mi bebé!*"

Reina Maria hears several pairs of feet shuffling toward her. Henry calls in the window.

"Does he have any fever? *Tiene calentura?*"

"*Si, tiene, tiene mucho calor!*"

Henry unlocks the chicken coop and quickly herds mother and baby out.

"Let me have the keys to your jeep, Jake, so's I can take them over to my place. Doc Chenoweth is near enough; I'll phone him on the way."

Jake frowns but hands him the keys. Pete says nothing, waiting till Reina Maria and Pacito are settled in the back of the jeep. Then he steps forward and grabs Henry by the forearm.

"Wait, Henry. Isn't this just the scene you were hell-bent on avoiding? Now you're moving a sick baby to your ranch, a baby that might die on the way in Jake's jeep, or on your property, in your house even."

"Well, don't tell me you want him to die in your chicken coop instead?" Henry says, moving toward the jeep. Pete blocks his way; his face tightens.

"No, I want him to die in a fucking Border Patrol car, and that's where I am taking them, to their patrol point down beyond Smith's ranch."

Pete grabs the keys from Henry, nudging him sideways, and hops into the driver's seat. Before anybody can say or do anything, he speeds off down the same road that Gilberto has walked several hours earlier. When he reaches the fork, he turns east, away from the *arroyo* that leads to the cabin, and then south again, back toward the border. The jeep thumps to a halt in a soft sand wash, under a large stand of cottonwoods.

Reina Maria has been knotted with terror, knowing that everything had gone wrong the moment Pete seized the keys. She has a good idea what is coming next, and squeezes Pacito tightly while her eyes flit wildly about, searching for a way out. From the back of the jeep, she can see Pete's belt. At his side, the pistol is still in its holster, his calloused fingers playing over the handle. But there is also a knife, folded into a leather pouch hanging at the back of his trousers. Before she can think enough to be afraid, she reaches forward, and in one smooth motion flicks open the snap, withdraws the knife, and pulls open its four-inch blade. Pete feels her touch and turns quickly around, damning her to hell and grabbing the arm she raises to shield herself and Pacito, who is clinging to her dress. Pete means to drag her from the jeep but as he rises from his seat, pulling the woman and child with him, Reina Maria thrusts wildly with her free hand and the knife slides through his shirt and into his side. He releases her arm and stares down as the blood pulses into his plaid shirt. Groaning in surprised pain, he grasps uselessly at his soaking side while Reina Maria jumps from the jeep with Pacito and without even glancing in Pete's direction, runs between the trees, away from the road and into the thickening vegetation of the secret riverbed, the knife still welded to her hand, clutching Pacito to her breast.

Soon she finds herself on the other side of the thicket, entering a wide expanse of thinning grasslands and, seeing no one following, begins to walk slowly through the desert night. She will come to a single-strand barbed wire fence and pass Pacito through and then follow herself. Back into Mexico. On the other side, she will straighten up, letting the knife fall to the earth, and look out across the brightening landscape. There will be a wide dirt road a few hundred yards ahead and possibly a ride to somewhere.

It has been dark for several hours when Gil finally gives up any hope that she will come to him. He makes his way quickly back to the fork in the road, standing under a thin crescent moon and listening for the sound of an engine in the still night.

It is nearly dawn when truck lights pierce the ebbing darkness and then slow as they make out Gilberto's shape walking wearily north along the ranch road. A truckload of ranch hands on their way home, and only too happy to pull Gilberto up over the side before rattling the several miles to their plywood homes and pots of steaming beans. He says nothing of where he's been. Or of who he is. Or was. Nor of the woman and child over whom he hopes San Francisco is watching.

8

The Tunnel

Fig. 8.1 Photograph by Maeve Hickey

© The Author(s) 2020
L. J. Taylor, *Tales from the Desert Borderland*, Palgrave Studies in Literary Anthropology, https://doi.org/10.1007/978-3-030-35133-5_8

They were in the tunnel. Ernesto, Chango, and La Negra.

Andando. Nosotros batos locos. Sí mon.

Still stoned from last night, they rest on the concrete shelf, watching the shallow chocolate water roll along beneath their dangling feet. La Negra complains that they are out of dope and Ernesto reaches into the depths of the low-slung, baggy jeans hanging damp around his legs and pulls out a spray can.

"*Oro. ¡La mejor!*"

He whispers into the echoing chamber and shakes the can tenderly so that they can hear each tantalizing echoing clink of the metal balls within. Chango hands him an empty Coke can. Ernesto takes graceful aim and sprays the gold paint inside, then passes it to his own Negra, who brings the can up to her bright red lips and huffs deeply. The stinging fumes circle in the back of her mouth and then burn their way up through her nose, exploding into the empty space behind her eyes.

"*¡Que me ponga loca! ¡Yo, La Negra!*"

Her arm, now floating of its own accord, finds Chango, who lifts the can gently from her hand and takes a hit, breathing in the cool, fetid dankness of the tunnel along with the paint fumes. Now Ernesto huffs, drawing more deeply than the others. To show strength. To seek oblivion.

A damp shuffling of footsteps echoes behind them, near the entrance. A consequential noise in the still, black chamber.

Ernesto frowns and whispers,

"*Ándale, batos locos. ¡A ver quién entra el barrio!*"

Together they are unafraid, cat-stepping back along the concrete walkway toward the entrance, pausing again when they hear a soft sloshing noise. Falling to hands and knees, they creep around the bend. Below them is the pool of water that has gathered at the tunnel bottom, near enough the entrance that a soft daylight plays on its surface, and on the pinched brown buttocks of a boy who is bent over in the water, rubbing a chunk of soap on a pair of jeans and slapping them around on the concrete.

Had he been bigger, they would have jumped him, but looking at his frail, naked form gleaming above the water, so busy with his laundry, it is all they can do to keep from laughing.

They rise to their feet and La Negra bellows, "Who in this motherfucking world are you, *putito*, and what do you think you are doing in our tunnel?"

The boy nearly topples over as he spins around to face the voice, covering himself with his sopping jeans. Chango and Ernesto laugh heartily, but La Negra stands there, hands on hips, glowering: a demon goddess, ebony face wide and wild-eyed, her hair long and glinting even in the weak light. She looks furious, but of course she is only play acting. Though with enough paint fumes this act fools herself as well as her audience. Soon, La Negra too is laughing with easy disdain at the cowering figure.

"*Mi casa es tu casa. ¿Cuántos años tienes?*"

The boy whispers that he is twelve. He looks ten and a small ten at that. He is there, he tells them in nervous gulps that soon settle into a quavering bravado, to wash his clothes and to maybe sleep right there. Near the entrance. Not really in the tunnel, which he knows is theirs. In fact, (by now he smiles hopefully), he wanted to meet them and maybe help with what he has heard is their work.

"*Sí mon, trabajaba con una pareja gringa, cruzando los chuntaros en el desierto. ¡Soy Lalo, copilota, navegador!*"

La Negra and Ernesto look unimpressed, but the boy, Lalo, rattles on, retrieving a frayed map of Arizona from a pile of clothing on the embankment. He unfolds it at their feet and moves his finger over the surface with authority, telling of his adventures helping to cross a trailer-load of *chuntaros* through the deadly desert.

"*¡No necesitamos ninguno pinche mapa o guía!*" La Negra spits out, "who needs maps to their own terreno?"

Ernesto, his voice echoing in the chamber, recites with some grandeur

"*Somos El Barrio Libre, y nuestro barrio es el túnel.*"

The tunnel is their home; its dark passage, like its sounds and smells, is inscribed in their souls. But Chango, dark with a droop eye that belies his quick mind, likes the idea of a map. He motions the others to follow him out into the daylight. Squatting in the soft dust, he takes up a stick and scratches lines into the dirt. Lalo watches rapt, Ernesto blinks in the daylight, and La Negra frowns, but leans over to add corrections as needed. When it is done, Chango's map shows two tunnels, running alongside one another, beginning where they stand, a couple of miles south of the border, in the heart of Nogales, Sonora. He draws a heavy line crossway over the tunnels: *La Línea*. The Border. But the tunnels continue across, under, that line to "*la Salida*" well into the other Nogales, in Arizona. *Ambos* Nogales—both Nogales—as people say there. Chango adds little boxes near the American end—the library and Church's Fried Chicken.

So it is that Lalo finds his home, like others of the most ragged and least anchored street kids of Nogales. "*Somos muchos*," Ernesto likes to say. At seventeen, he is an elder with six years on and under the streets of Nogales. He is a leader as long as he acts the part with cool competence. To look sure of himself and of his girl, La Negra, even when he is not. Especially when he is not. To be singular and at the same time, many—*muchos*. There are indeed dozens of these denizens of the deep, citizens of the subterranean nation. But within that nation, the lost children make little makeshift, fragile families whose less abstract love is borne of shared sleep, food, and sometimes bodies. In shared need and hope.

Most came on their own like Ernesto, who at ten, when his mother's latest boyfriend kicked him out of their shack in the colonias of Guadalajara, peddled pills in the streets for several years until he heard about the opportunities of the border. Clinging to steel bars between freight cars for the two-day trip he came to Nogales, where he slept in fields and abandoned cars until he met his new brothers.

So, Lalo has found his barrio beyond the barrios. There will be no initiation, no spilled blood. The only mark he will bear is a simple homemade tattoo on his slight wrist: three ink dots in a triangle, "*mi vida loca*." The crazy life of El Barrio Libre. And he will learn to dance his belonging with his hands, sweeping gestured letters: B and L. El Barrio Libre.

Who hang together.

Sí mon.

Who toke together.

Ándale.

Who steal and survive together.

Órale.

And Lalo has found his family with Ernesto, Chango, and La Negra. For the boys he will be a pet, one Ernesto sometimes loses patience with but in whom Chango recognizes agility of mind as well as body. Of course, all three boys are enamored of La Negra, who plays the difficult lover for Ernesto and the playful tease to Chango. With Lalo she will be the rough, caressing older sister, and, even at ten, he will receive her attention with more innocence than he feels.

* * *

Across the line, in the other Nogales, Orozco squirms restlessly on the new brocade sofa. Leonora loves their new split-level on the edge of the golf course, but he has yet to feel at home. He flicks the remote, irritated by the endless pre-game nonsense. Leonora looks at him as she passes the open doorway between the kitchen and the living room, happy to see him finally relaxing. At home. Watching the game. Normal.

Except that he is alone. Hard to understand why, back here in Nogales where they had grown up surrounded by people, in lives seamless across time and space, and the border. Naturally, she had encouraged him to apply for the position.

"Who is better qualified than you to be commander?"

"They'll never do it. Never put a man in charge of his own home place. Not where so much is going on, Illegals, drugs, money. Someone with too many local connections just doesn't look good. Believe me, they are gonna put in some young guy from Wisconsin with a couple of college degrees. And the title is PAIC. Patrol Agent in Charge."

She couldn't understand what she knew was really his own reluctance to apply. And "commander" was what she and her friends were going to say.

Reluctant as he may have been to take the job, Orozco wasn't long vanishing into it. He was determined to prove himself beyond reproach but equally anxious to do more than implement directives from Tucson. After all, he knew the place: where and how people and contraband move across the border, and in some cases the people doing it. Hadn't he gone to school on the Arizona side with many of them? So, Orozco increased patrols, gathered better intelligence, and moved surveillance cameras and sensors, repositioning them regularly and randomly, a step ahead of the enemy. Very soon his men were no longer the laughable *"chiles verdes,"* always just missing their mark. No, they were always right there, parked in the shadows waiting: in the hillside neighborhoods of Nogales, Arizona, along the ranch roads, out in the desert. Orozco dominated his border, closing it down and cinching it up as it had never been before.

Leonora pours the bowl of diced potatoes into the sputtering oil and then steps back from the stove to where she can see her husband. She wonders how a man that big can somehow look like a bored child, though his face does seem more haggard lately, his mustache grayer. Does he still find her attractive at fifty? She catches her own reflection in the glass of the wall oven, still smooth mocha skin, clear eyes, but she has been putting on weight since their return: at least a pound or two for every relative they have, whose photographs clutter every wall and surface with the sole exception of the sofa end tables, each of which supports a lamp in the shape of the Mexican Coat-of-Arms: a rampant eagle clutching a serpent atop a nopal cactus.

Heavier, but certainly happier. She was delighted to come home as the wife of the "Commander," to click-clack over the border to help at her Cousin Alma's jewelry shop, to be asked to serve as Democratic Committee lady. Friends suggested that she might run for City Council. When she enters a local restaurant, she doesn't reach her seat before at least half the patrons have risen to greet her, ladies appraising her dress and men taking her hand, and everyone asking after her family.

She slides the folded tortillas—each one now filled with fried potatoes and a generous pinch of Santa Cruz Chili powder—back into the oil.

Orozco picks up the local paper and just to further annoy himself, reads a story aloud to Leonora. Another tale of doped-up gang kids popping up and mugging some poor bastard making his way from Church's Fried Chicken and then disappearing back into their vile hole. The *pinche* tunnel. Beneath his feet the great, painful exception to his control, dug decades before to drain the summer rains from Nogales Sonora, taking the flow under the border and into the Santa Cruz River. On this border, the waters flow like everything else, from south to north. These days, the tunnels carry more than water.

Against her better judgment Leonora asks,

"Why doesn't the Patrol just sit on the exit there and catch everybody coming out?"

He looks up with the tired annoyance that comes with giving the same answer to an endlessly posed question.

"Because it's like putting a cork in the spout of a boiling tea kettle without turning off the flame. They will find other ways out. They crawl along the smaller side passages and into storm drains all over town, they come up through sewer grates, they burst through sidewalks with floor jacks. They bring drugs up through trap doors. Closing the tunnel never works. If you wall it up completely, Nogales, Sonora will spend the summer under water. You know what happened when they put the metal grates in. Supposed to let water through, but not people. First heavy rains the grates are plastered with wood, tires, everything. Trash dams! Floods again. OK, so that idiot chief, Walker, puts in retractable grates. Within a week the damned narcos had torched them out of there. So, it's a free for all down there and now the illegals are moving through too. Led by their *polleros*. Or even by those filthy kids living down there, when they aren't doping and robbing."

Orozco drops the paper on the coffee table.

Leonora, who stopped listening after the first sentence, changes the subject.

"I'm nervous about what to serve at the Democratic fund-raiser next week. Jane says you must have shrimp for that kind of occasion. She says she will drive up to Sam's Club in Tucson to get a few of their prepared trays."

Orozco screws up his face.

"Sam's Club? Use some real *camerones* from Guaymas for God's sake! Your cousin can bring them up. We can grill them."

Leonora smiles as she sets down the tray in front of him. She hoped he would say that. He will insist on grilling them himself and he is a happy man when bending into a smoking fire, lecturing anyone nearby on the art of barbecue.

She takes a quick look out the window at the ominous clouds gathering as they do nearly every afternoon this time of summer and worries what the weather will be for the fund-raiser. She sighs but can't help but smile as she nudges the tray heavy with glistening, golden-brown treats toward her husband.

"Your favorite, *doraditos*. Have a few now but leave some for later when Ophelia and the baby come by. Maybe she'll bring Robert to watch the game with you."

Leonora moves back into the kitchen, leaving Orozco to crunch and stare at the TV. The players are finally running out onto the field, but now he is wondering if he can hide cameras in the tunnel, not just near the American exit, but deep inside, by the unmarked border. And maybe even get one of the gear heads at work to rig things so he could pick up the transmissions on his TV at home.

* * *

Reina Maria and her baby had gotten a lift with pilgrims returning from Magdalena to Nogales. She didn't have to tell them who she was or where she was going. They let her out at the edge of a park in the center of the city and told her to wait on a bench under a towering bronze statue representing some revolutionary person or abstract ideal. A *coyote* or *pollero* would find her there.

The park is a thin strip of almost quiet green amid the rattling chaos of the city. The north/south avenues on either side are choked with smoking, honking traffic, a least of third of which seems to be pickups stenciled with the insignia of one or another enforcement agency and loaded with armed men in matching T-shirts. The *colonias* stretch up the hillsides to the east and west, narco mansions scattered willy-nilly among the ragged shacks. People and animals pass among the houses along steep paths and crumbling outdoor stairways. The whole sorry mess looks ready to tumble and slide at the slightest provocation.

She gives the baby, Pacito, her breast and, with some difficulty stops thinking about the man with whom she had passed the night in the desert. No. She will find her husband and brothers in the place written on the paper. She will tell them only some things about her passage as they will surely only tell her some things about their own.

Vagrants and thugs drift about in the park, every one of them looking mean enough to be a *pollero*, but it is the least likely one who approaches: a ragged little boy wearing a baseball cap, baggy pants, a silver chain bouncing on a skinny, bare chest, and a silly grin.

"*Soy Lalo. Quieres cruzar, ¿Verdad? ¿Porque no vienes con nosotros?*"

His face is smudged with dried mud, but Lalo has a disarming grin that says, "you'd only laugh at any mischief I'd be up to." He darts back across the street, disappearing into dense cloud of rotisserie smoke that is rising under a giant, inanely laughing chicken head: "El Pollo Feliz," and then returns in short order with La Negra, as dark as Reina Maria, but tall and athletic, with thick Indian hair, large red lips and cunning black eyes. Her red T-shirt billows slightly in the evening breeze. There is only a hint of toughness in the little twist of her mouth as the smile melts away, leaving the impenetrable deadpan of the border streets. Looking intently at Reina Maria, La Negra smiles again and reaches out to smooth away a sticky lock of hair from the baby's eye, speaking to the young mother and child.

"*Pues sí, les cruzamos a ustedes.*"

Reina Maria feels the baby's hot breath against her neck. Fighting a lifetime habit, she forces herself to look directly into the girl's eyes, seeking a sign of the betrayal she feels sure will follow. As it always has.

Ernesto and Chango are across the street washing windshields at the traffic light. They prance out into the street whenever the light turns red, armed with buckets of sudsy water, squeegees and deeply soiled rags. Masters of their trade, they are never pathetic, never imploring or desperate. They approach each car, and most especially those of the gringos, with bonhomie and confidence, like favored workers in amiable service to a respected client. And they take absolutely no notice of the mostly wagging heads or fingers, or of the condition of the car. No, it doesn't matter whether it is dirty enough to have several weeks of love messages fingered into the dusty surface, or glistening, just washed, in the sun. Only if the car is somber and mean, with windows blackened against the sun and prying eyes, do they wait until invited. Otherwise, it is the joyful splash and masterly wipe for every vehicle. Any coin is blessed with bows and laughs, and curses are offered to the tight-fisted assholes who speed away.

They abandon their washing station to cross the street and take their positions behind La Negra, fanning out around Reina Maria and Pacito. Feigning the ease of confident possession, Ernesto sits away from La Negra, throwing his long dark arms out around the shoulders of the boys seated at his sides. His boys: Chango and little Lalo.

Reina Maria of course doesn't feel inclined to risk her baby and her own life with a gang of street kids. She knows this "cholo" act, for it reaches all the way south to her part of the country. Yet another set of hungry eyes. No wonder they call us *pollos*. We are chickens.

But she asks,

"How will we go? How long will it take?"

"We go through our *barrio, hermanita,* the tunnel. It's only a couple of miles."

La Negra says this with a grin.

"But dangerous miles, *¿verdad?* We must be paid for that danger, so it will cost you three hundred dollars. A bargain, right?"

They are all smiling. Children, then vaguely threatening, then children again. Reina Maria is about to say no but pauses to consider her options. She looks up again to see La Negra fondly tousling Pacito's hair and little Lalo looking like her own little brother, Victór.

She tells them she has only two hundred.

La Negra is about to insist on three when Ernesto rises and saunters over to her side, laying a long-fingered hand on La Negra's shoulder.

"For the sake of the little one, he says, looking at Pacito, who returns his brown-eyed stare, we'll do it for two hundred. Won't we?"

He is wondering if the woman is foolish enough to offer all her money for the crossing, leaving her to venture penniless into the other side.

La Negra feels a flash of anger at Ernesto. This little one looks too much like their own Carlita, and he doesn't seem to be thinking of her very often.

* * *

Orozco squints into the damp gloom. Dykstra and Villaseñor hang back a few yards, guns drawn, hating the crap detail they have been given, and hating Orozco for giving it to them. It only makes it worse that he's come along himself. There is plenty of headroom, but the two agents crouch, as if to diminish their presence. Tentative. Temporary. Ready and willing to leave, as are the two workers just behind them, who have come unhappily along to install the camera, and are increasingly nervous as they move farther into the tunnel. Orozco, however, stands bolt upright in reproach, pacing steadily ahead checking his Global Positioning System.

Above them, what look like tiny ceiling lights are spots of daylight finding their way through the regular spaces in the road paving above. In the bending distance the lights are reduced to pinpricks in the blackness, illuminating nothing. The men can hear a nauseating sloshing and tinkling beneath them, though from where they stand on the concrete embankment that projects from both sides of the tunnel, the water at the bottom seems still, thick and lumpy. The smell of urine is overpowering.

"Here."

Orozco nods at Villaseñor, who approaches with a chalk line and a can of spray paint.

Once the line is made, Orozco indicates the spot, a few yards farther back, where the workers are to install the camera, set into the wall and covered over with a rusty steel plate so that it looks as if it had always been there. They are finished and more than ready to leave, but Orozco takes his time, admiring the work: his camera, his line. He is a field marshal surveying an ominously silent battlefield whose name will be linked with his own for generations.

It is only on the way back, as they more quickly traverse the few hundred yards to the tunnel exit, that Orozco thinks of his daughter, Ophelia, and the turmoil she has wrought by turning up with the child, a suitcase and no husband. And no explanation. Leonora said that he would have to draw her out, find out what happened. But what chance would he have on that front? Besides, there was nothing he could do to change his work schedule. The camera had arrived. The workers were already scheduled for the installation. He had to go. It was easy enough to read her eyes: frustrated, accusing. Didn't she too have work that couldn't be rescheduled? The fund-raiser was the next day, and the damned tunnel would always be there. Doesn't family come first? But she said nothing.

* * *

In the night they sleep in a tiny, cave-like space within the crumbling walls of the old bullfight stadium: Ernesto, Chango, Lalo, La Negra, and the mother and child. The cholos are wedged together on a sheet of old cardboard and Reina Maria leans up against the wall with Pacito in her lap, desperately tired and yet too fearful to sleep. Beyond the walls she can hear the near and distant rustling of countless others; she feels like stunned prey dragged by vicious insects into one among countless cells that comprise their chambered nest. But she emerges alive into a clear Saturday morning, with none of the dark clouds that have threatened and sometimes opened these past days. Lalo has returned from the Pollo Feliz where his table-wiping was rewarded with a day-old roasted chicken and a pile of stale corn tortillas. Chango sets about doling out the food, pulling bits of chicken from the bony carcass and wrapping them in the small tortillas. He hands a fistful to Ernesto and La Negra, who are still slumped in the dark corner of their shelter. Another couple for little Lalo. And then a neat pile stacked on a soiled paper plate for Reina Maria and her child. He stoops onto the rocky ground alongside them, smiling wanly. Reina Maria, who has been afraid to look directly into Chango's droopy eye now sees a shy kindness there and then, behind it, a near wisdom. He is no more than fourteen, but his hands seem older—years of picking chiles in damp fields beyond Obregon followed by the rough life and work of the streets and tunnels.

"*De donde eres?*"

Reina Maria is startled at the first question she has been asked since her passage was secured.

She tells Chango something of her pueblo in Chiapas, and he surprises her again by asking her about her own people, the *Maya*. For he too has another language—or at least his parents did—from the hills above and beyond the fields in which all the family labored alongside their fellow *Yaquis*, living now in rows of thatch-roofed workers' shacks, working and getting poorer, working and becoming Mexican. It is a conversation he has never had with Ernesto or La Negra.

* * *

The fund-raiser is underway. Orozco is manning the barbeque, his determined face shining with sweat as he fusses with the skewers of shrimp, dabbing them with more crimson oil and rolling them one at a time to offer up a new surface to be licked by the jumping flames. The grill is set on the edge of a flagstone patio. Beyond is the lawn, stretching green and uninterrupted to the back fence—a conceit that could persist through the drier months only with constant vigilance against the encroaching desert, always ready to reassert itself.

Leonora is happy to see him absorbed, knowing that it will improve her husband's mood, or at least mask his visible disappointment with Ophelia, whom she is attempting and failing to distract by bringing her to guest after guest, the whole time dragging the toddler, who has a desperate hold on her leg. Ophelia has been thinking only about the creep of a husband she finally left. She wishes him dead. But she looks up at each new person entering the garden, hoping it will be him, haggard and sorry. Begging her to come home.

"Since you're here, I'd love a hand with these. Maybe the baby can play with her doll for a while?"

Ophelia is surprised to find a tray of hors d'oeuvres pushed into her hands: the pallid crackers with squirts of green paste that Jane Rentmeister, who is hovering nearby, insisted on providing.

"That's a family secret! The green paste."

Ophelia smiles distractedly, not sure if her mother's friend is joking, but Leonora laughs loudly enough that Orozco looks up from the grill, happy that his daughter and wife are getting along, but hoping that the bastard husband shows up some time soon to reclaim his family. He turns the skewered shrimps, noting with approval the nicely blackened marinade, a paste of garlic, chile, and lemon.

Then the first drops of rain hiss on the hot coals.

* * *

Reina Maria shoulders her baby and follows the *cholos* into the tunnel entrance. The sound of the traffic above dies away as they pass between walls boldly tagged with dozens of names—living and dead, in prison and still-at-large—including those of Ernesto, Chango, and La Negra. Lalo too has added his own, a backward-leaning comic book script.

Ernesto and Chango lead the way and little Lalo and La Negra walk behind the pollos. La Negra watches Pacito, thinking again of Carlita, who is nearly the same age, now living with her *pinche hermana en la Colonia Solidaridad*. "Your sister can give her a better life." That's all her father had to say when the bitch from Child Welfare took Carlita away. He just sat there, thin and broken by work, wearing the shameful horns his wife had put on him when she ran away with the dope dealer, happy enough that one daughter was working in a fucking *maquiladora* and living in a tidy shack with electricity and a boyfriend who also worked, and done caring about his other daughter. A*ndando loca en los túneles*. But why shouldn't she go into the street, out of that suffocating *pinche* house with the ball-less father who wouldn't just watch the baby for her? He had to fucking give her away to her bitch sister. How can Carlita be better off? Doesn't she feel the same pain in her gut? Doesn't she miss being passed from lap to lap and carried, always gurgling happily, on Chango's shoulders as they troop through the streets of Nogales. Ernesto was going to be a better father than hers, and he would love her forever. Like in the songs. The songs. If she could only live in the songs. If she could hold on to some money, she could rent a place better than her sister's, find a job better than her sister's, and get her baby back.

Reina Maria turns to look at La Negra, feeling her eyes, perhaps seeking some reassurance. But La Negra can give her none. She feels envy, hatred, even pity, but despises the woman's weakness. She will help them, but she wants her to lose her baby as she has hers.

* * *

"Do you think we need to move the party inside?" Leonora asks Orozco.

She has prepared for the contingency but would very much prefer to keep things going out in the back yard. Orozco surveys the skies. Above them the streak of gray cloud that wept a few drops has already drifted farther to the east. A few miles south a dense black thunderhead is gathering into itself. But it is not moving their way.

"You'll be ok for a couple hours anyway; more than you need."

As Leonora turns back to her guests, beaming and determined to beat the weather, Orozco's cell phone rings.

"Thought you'd want to know, chief, the new sensors are picking up something moving through the tunnel. The camera isn't showing anything yet, but Maggie is glued to the screen here at the station."

Leonora is watching her husband's face as he talks on the phone and, recognizing the tense smile knows that whatever he is being told is about work and far more interesting than her event.

"Get Dykstra and meet me at the entrance in five minutes and tell Maggie to keep in touch."

* * *

In the sheltered deep of the tunnel none can hear the thunder or watch the blackening sky. Above, the first drops fall on the corrugated roofs, held down with tires, bricks, even wheelbarrows and bicycles, high in *Colonia Luis Donaldo Colosio*. They gain momentum quickly, now pattering noisily on the tin, slurring into the dust, running into one another and streaming along the cracked and crumbling stairways and pathways, down the steep hillsides into the low-lying *avenidas*, already laden with wood scraps, bras, and sunbaked goat turds. Below, these streams meet and marry others, each on its way down from one of the many other hillside barrios, following the dirt channels carved into the earth by previous rains. Now they form angry rivers, surging northward, planks, tires, and shopping carts swirling and bobbing along for the ride.

"*Da me tu dinero.*"

La Negra stands in front of Reina Maria, away from the others, who have paused behind them to pass around a joint. She fingers the knife in her pocket, sure that she won't need to use it, but liking the feeling. Reina Maria hands over the $200, but the ease with which she does so makes La Negra, who is high and both angered and comforted by the young mother, by her baby, by her hope, believe that Reina Maria has more. Much more.

"*Da me todo que tenga, hermanita.*"

She hears herself say this while drawing the knife slowly from her pocket, a wolf mother, convinced that she will use every penny for her own child. Thinking that maybe this bitch has many hundreds of dollars, enough to rent an apartment. To start a life. To get Carlita back. Why is the woman not answering, not moving? Chango, hearing the pitch of La Negra's voice gives the joint back to Ernesto and moves toward the girls.

* * *

By the time Orozco's cell phone buzzes in his pocket, they are within the tunnel, only fifty yards from "the border." There is instead a grim determination in his stride, whether confident or fatalistic it is difficult to know. Dykstra and Villaseñor follow slowly behind, all too accustomed to his campaigns.

It's Maggie, back at the station.

"They're in the camera, there. Mostly teens, I'd say. Tunnel rats. But wait ... there's a baby. Yeah, one of them is holding a baby."

They fall to their knees, weapons ready. Villaseñor hefts the reassuring weight of his pistol, remembering that the kids are rarely armed with anything but knives, Dykstra feels like he is about to throw up, and Orozco stares straight ahead, smiling tensely, resolute. The tunnel is his. He can just make out some sheets of soiled cardboard, ragged blankets, and empty paint spray cans. Beyond all that there are voices, so low they nearly merge with the echoing slur of the water.

* * *

La Negra is about to insist, this time with the knife that lies in the palm of her hand, that Reina Maria turn over every cent on her body. Everything. Then she will strip her bare, convinced now that this woman is the only thing standing between herself and her own baby. Maybe the baby the woman carries is really Carlita. La Negra hears her own thoughts like insistent voices, like she hears the roar of her own blood coursing through her ears. A roar that echoes outside now, louder and louder, like a freight train, crashing through the tunnel behind them.

"¡Agua! ¡Agua!"

Lalo and the others are running toward them, shouting. When La Negra turns to hear them, Reina Maria, clutching Pacito to her chest, breaks into a panicky run ahead through the dark passage. Suddenly, she sees men rise like spirits from the shadows. Men in uniforms. With guns. Guns pointed at her. But behind her, the roar is deafening.

As indiscriminate as a biblical punishment, the fearsome river has found the tunnel. turbulent, dark and ugly, it has scoured the passages and carries the flotsam and jetsam of the Nogales streets and alleys.

Bobbing tires and scraps of wood. Blankets, plastic jugs, and tumbling spray cans. A churning wall of water, breaking, dragging under, tossing up, surges across the line spray-painted on the dank concrete and carries all before it.

Proud Ernesto,
Wily Chango,
Little Lalo,
Beautiful Negra,
Reina Maria and tiny Pacito,
Dykstra, Villasenor,
Orozco.
On through the darkened passage and into the United States.

CPI Antony Rowe
Eastbourne, UK
March 11, 2020